3-MINUTE
DEVOTIONS
for Moms

of Little Ones

© 2018 by Barbour Publishing, Inc.

Compiled and edited by Courtney Coffman.

Print ISBN 978-1-68322-251-4

Portions of this book previously appeared in *Daily Whispers of Wisdom for Mothers of Preschoolers*, published by Barbour Publishing.

Published by Barbour Books, an imprint of Barbour Publishing, Inc., 1810 Barbour Drive, Uhrichsville, Ohio 44683, www.barbourbooks.com

Our mission is to inspire the world with the life-changing message of the Bible.

Member of the
Evangelical Christian
Publishers Association

Printed in the United States of America.

3-MINUTE
DEVOTIONS
for Moms
of Little Ones

BARBOUR BOOKS
An Imprint of Barbour Publishing, Inc.

Introduction

Nobody has to tell a mother of a little one that her job is a tough one. You're already well aware of that.

What you might need to hear, though, are some regular reminders of God's love for you. . .of the vital importance of the job you're doing. . .of the incredible blessings of motherhood in spite of the daily struggles. That's what *3-Minute Devotions for Moms of Little Ones* is all about—providing simple encouragement to help you face your challenges with confidence, hope, even joy. Here's how to use this book in 3 short minutes:

- Minute 1: Reflect on God's Word

- Minute 2: Read real-life application and encouragement

- Minute 3: Pray

These devotions aren't meant to be a replacement for digging deep into the scriptures or for personal, in-depth quiet time. Instead, consider them a perfect jump start to help you form a habit of spending time with God every day—especially in the midst of busy mommyhood! Be blessed, Mom!

*And they blessed Rebekah, and said unto her, Thou art
our sister, be thou the mother of thousands of millions, and
let thy seed possess the gate of those which hate them.*

GENESIS 24:60 KJV

In Rebekah's day, children were considered a blessing from God. Rebekah's family didn't actually expect her to give birth to that many children. They were simply asking God to bless her new family.

Children are God's blessing to you. Whether you have one child or many, you have a unique opportunity to influence the world. As a Christian mother, you can instill your faith in your children while they are still young. As they grow, they will have the chance to witness to those you might never meet, and the process will continue.

Rebekah only bore two children—nowhere close to "thousands of millions." But one of her sons was Jacob—the father of Christ's bloodline. Rebekah was blessed indeed, and so are you. That's something to keep in mind as you go through your day.

---

*Dear Lord, You have blessed me with beautiful
children and a special opportunity to influence many people.
Help me take this responsibility to heart. Amen.*

Blessing vs. Cursing

From the same mouth come both blessing and cursing.
JAMES 3:10 NASB

"How many times do I have to tell you?"

"Children are to be seen and not heard."

"Sit down!"

"Don't chew with your mouth open."

These sayings will pierce the hearts of young children when they continually hear belittling comments or corrections stemming from anger and frustration.

God gives us one mouth that we can use to speak blessings or curses over our children. None of us would intentionally speak curses over our children, but every time we belittle, demean, or speak words of correction out of anger and not love, we are cursing them.

We are God's children, loved and chosen for the purpose of glorifying Him in all we say and do. We are coheirs with Christ, saved, and blessed. We can correct our children with patience, love, kindness, and God's truth. We can remind our children—and ourselves—of these truths with words of blessing versus cursing.

Lord, please guard my mouth to speak words of blessing to my children. Help me to hear Your words of blessing and then speak those blessings to my children. Amen.

Meant to Be Broken?

*If thou shalt hearken diligently unto the voice of the
Lord thy God, to observe and to do all his commandments...
all these blessings shall come on thee, and overtake thee.*

DEUTERONOMY 28:1–2 KJV

We've all heard the phrase "Rules were made to be broken."
Our young children prove this concept all the time. However,
their rule breaking is sometimes innocent curiosity rather
than intentional disregard for our instruction.

The rules we set in place—like not crossing the street
without an adult and not eating candy before dinner—are
not meant to make our children miserable. Instead, they're
meant to do the opposite: keep them safe and happy.

God has similar expectations for us as adults. We may
not understand why the rules are in place, but we know that
God, our loving Father, means them for our good, to keep us
safe and happy.

As you walk with the Lord today, remember that God
is watching you and leading you, ready to fill your life with
blessings as you walk in His will, His way.

*Lord, thank You for keeping me safe, and for
blessing my life as I strive to follow You. Amen.*

In His Steps

*For even hereunto were ye called: because Christ
also suffered for us, leaving us an example,
that ye should follow his steps.*

1 PETER 2:21 KJV

We know that Christ understands all that we go through, but sometimes we make decisions without first turning to Him for direction. We want our children to develop Christlikeness in their lives, but they are watching *us*. They will quickly develop "mom-likeness." If our desire is that they become more like Jesus, we must be willing to be like Him ourselves.

Yes, mothers need to be tough in certain situations, but too often that develops into the do-it-myself mentality. Instead, it should be an I-can-do-it-through-Christ mentality. What a joy to follow the footsteps that our Savior has left us. What a blessing to realize our children are choosing to walk in those same steps.

You are naturally going to be one of your child's first role models. What kind will you be? There are many options, but it is best to be one who looks to Jesus as her own role model.

---

*Thank You, Jesus, for leaving Your footsteps for me to follow.
Help me to never take them for granted. Amen.*

Blowing Off the Blues

A merry heart maketh a cheerful countenance:
but by sorrow of the heart the spirit is broken.
PROVERBS 15:13 KJV

Mothers of young children often experience "the blues," from childbirth all the way through the "terrible twos," "trying threes," and "frustrating fours"! When little Jeremiah flushes his shoes down the toilet and Kiara decorates the walls with lipstick just before company arrives, Mom feels like throwing in the towel.

The best antidote for the blues? A break—even a short one. A quick snooze while the kids nap, or a let-off-steam phone call to an understanding friend can make all the difference.

A mom can also jump-start her joy. Watching a silly video with her children or drawing fun pictures together might help heal a morning of aggravation. Best of all, Mom can ask God to help her see the comic side of life. The Lord of Laughter wants to cultivate humor in her heart that will lift her head, brighten her face, and strengthen her spirit!

Loving Father, how can You parent millions of people 24-7?
You must possess an amazing sense of humor.
Please share a few of Your smiles with me today. Amen.

The Great Physician

*Praise the LORD, my soul, and forget not all his benefits—
who forgives all your sins and heals all your diseases.*

PSALM 103:2-3 NIV

One of the realities of motherhood is that your child will experience health ailments. Common colds, stomach viruses, and countless other illnesses can strike at any time.

As a mom, it is difficult to stand vigil at the bedside of a suffering child. It takes a toll physically, as you console around the clock. It is also mentally draining, as at 3:00 a.m. you try to recall the last time you administered fever-reducing medicine.

Many moms offer a silent prayer in these moments of distress, but the next time you're faced with a medical crisis, pray *with* your child. Sickness is a reality of life, but we know the One who has created our bodies and has the power to heal them. By suggesting your child pray, he will learn to call on God and trust Him for healing in his body.

---

*Heavenly Father, I pray for my sick child.
Please restore him to full health, and give me the
strength I need as I care for him. Amen.*

Safe in Christ

For in the day of trouble he will
keep me safe in his dwelling.

PSALM 27:5 NIV

Crack! Boom! "Mommy, I'm scared!" the little girl cried as thunder clapped outside the window. Knowing that an explanation of the physics of static electricity would not alleviate her daughter's fears, the mother simply provided a safe haven from the storm.

The storms of life have a way of frightening us also. Perhaps an upcoming surgery or financial difficulties are looming overhead. Maybe marital stress or child-rearing issues have cast dark clouds over our homes. We may not understand what is happening, but the Lord tells us all we need to know: we are safe because He is with us.

Seek shelter from the storm. Run to the Lord's dwelling. He will keep you safe and grant you peace. Like thunder and lightning, the storms we face in life are temporary, but the Lord remains. We are eternally safe in His dwelling. Come in out of the storm.

Dear Lord, help me seek shelter from life's storms by coming to You. Thank You for keeping me safe and secure. Amen.

Walking with Christ

*As you therefore have received
Christ Jesus the Lord, so walk in Him.*
COLOSSIANS 2:6 NKJV

From the time they can walk on their own, toddlers want independence. They don't want to stay with Mom or hold her hand. Young children don't understand the dangers in maneuvering through a crowd or crossing a busy street. They just want to go their own way.

When we force them to hold our hand, they will pout or cry. They may see something exciting and ignore all danger signs. Like our children, we don't know the best direction to take. That is why God desires for us to walk close to Him, following His steps. He sees the dangers ahead or the temptations that can lead us astray. He wants to help us maneuver through life with a minimum of stress.

Jesus Christ set an example for us. When we are His, we are to walk with Him. We must stay close so that our focus is on Him, not on the worldly enticements that can lead to danger.

Thank You, Jesus, for leading the way. Help me keep close to Your side and always walk with You. Amen.

Walk in the Light

Come ye, and let us walk in the light of the LORD.
ISAIAH 2:5 KJV

Motherhood is a genuine pleasure for the most part, but there are times when it is frightening and confusing. Every good mother wants the best for her child, but there are many factors to consider when deciding what is "best." Once the little one joins the family, every choice the parents make will affect the child either directly or indirectly. There is no doubt that motherhood is a great responsibility.

Many women feel the urge to subscribe to every parenting magazine and purchase a library's worth of child-rearing books to help them in their quest to properly bring up their children. These publications often do contain helpful and encouraging information and suggestions, but they're much more useful if they are used along with God's Word. Walking in His light gives us confidence and strength to be the mothers God intends us to be. God wants us to find this a joyous time of life, and He has the answers.

Light of the World, please clear the fog of confusion and help me raise my children by the standards in Your Word. Amen.

Known By Heart

Study to shew thyself approved unto God, a workman that needeth not to be ashamed, rightly dividing the word of truth.

2 TIMOTHY 2:15 KJV

The mother smiled at her son's obvious delight in the story she was reading. As she finished the final page, he turned back to the beginning and begged her to read the tale again. She marveled that after three times through, he wanted to hear it again.

Later, the mother noted her child sitting by himself, staring at the pages of the book. He began to "read" the story by heart, turning the pages at the right place and pointing to the pictures as she had done.

We should never tire of reading God's Word. Each day we must pray for God to give us a new heart to hear what He has written to us. Our delight in His instructions and encouragement should be childlike awe.

Thank You, God, for Your living Word. Help me to memorize the scriptures and keep them in my heart. Amen.

What If?

*You can go to bed without fear; you will lie down
and sleep soundly. You need not be afraid of
sudden disaster or the destruction that comes
upon the wicked, for the LORD is your security.*

PROVERBS 3:24-26 NLT

Mothers often wake with their minds racing. Strange thoughts burst unbidden in their minds: Their daughter runs across the street and gets hit by a car. Their son falls off his bicycle and hurts his head. *What if these things really happen?* they wonder.

Such nagging worries are common to all moms. We know how helpless we are to guarantee that life turns out well for our little ones. Anxieties can hold us captive, preventing us from enjoying our children's risks and accomplishments. All we see are the risks. Not the delight of climbing a tree, only the danger of falling.

Scripture reminds us that there's no place our children can go where they are outside of God's care. God loves our children even more than we do. Remember, our confidence is in the Lord.

*Lord, help me accept the hazards of life, knowing that You
hold us in Your strong embrace for all eternity. Amen.*

Get Refreshed

*It is a sign between me and the children of Israel for
ever: for in six days the LORD made heaven and earth,
and on the seventh day he rested, and was refreshed.*

EXODUS 31:17 KJV

"I just vacuumed," the mother moaned. The carpet was now
covered with crumbs from a package of crackers her three-
year-old had discovered. She picked up the little boy and
carried him to his bed for a nap. It wasn't long before she
heard delighted squeals coming from his room. She went
to investigate only to discover another mess. It seemed her
darling child had squirreled away a purple crayon and was
now using his yellow walls as a canvas. The mother burst into
tears, grabbed the crayon, and stalked out of the room.

As moms, often we feel we are exempt from the need to
rest. We push until we collapse spiritually, physically, and
emotionally. We need to take God's example and make time
to rest.

---

*O God, I don't know how I have time to rest, but You rested.
If You know it's necessary, how can I refuse?
Help me find time to be refreshed. Amen.*

Jesus Loves Me

"Let the little children come to me, and do not hinder them. . . ." And he took the children in his arms, placed his hands on them and blessed them.

MARK 10:14, 16 NIV

It is music to the Lord's ears to hear His beloved children sing, talk about, and talk to Him. Jesus encouraged mothers to bring their children to Him. Picture Jesus with a huge smile and warm embrace, gathering the children up in His arms, praying for them, laughing with them. Jesus loves children. Our young ones are innocent and trustworthy. They believe what we tell them. Therefore, let's begin at an early age, telling them about the truth of their Lord. Through their attending Sunday school, singing praise songs and hymns, and saying short prayers to the Lord, our children will come to have a foundation that cannot be shaken. They will model for us the simple faith it takes to believe Jesus and know that Jesus loves them.

Lord, help me to teach my children about You. Enable me to have the childlike ability to trust You and take You at Your Word. Amen.

Childish Ways

When I was a child, I talked like a child, I thought like a child, I reasoned like a child. When I became a man, I put the ways of childhood behind me.

1 CORINTHIANS 13:11 NIV

As mothers, we desire that our children mature properly. Yet sometimes on their journey to adulthood, we do not allow them to be children. We expect them to be grown up and leave childish ways behind. Adulthood will come soon enough. Do not try to rush the process by putting unrealistic demands on them. Learn to major on the majors and minor on the minors by seeking the Lord's discernment. Ask the question "Does this issue have eternal significance?" If the answer is no, allow your child to talk, think, and reason like a child. As an adult, they will be expected to put those childish ways behind them. Until then, let them be a kid!

Dear Lord, I confess that sometimes I want my child to behave as an adult. Give me Your wisdom and discernment. Amen.

Out of the Mouths of Babes

Through the praise of children and infants you have established a stronghold against your enemies, to silence the foe and the avenger.

PSALM 8:2 NIV

A little girl accompanied her grandmother to the mall's food court after attending Bible study together. As they were eating, the granddaughter noticed a boy holding a Burger King figurine. She excitedly exclaimed, "Look! Baby Jesus!" The grandmother recalled the children's story that morning: "Wise Men Visit Baby Jesus." At three years old, her granddaughter understood!

Children are like sponges; they take in the contents of their environment. Their minds quickly absorb. Their hearts openly receive. Therefore, every effort should be made to teach them God's truths.

You may believe that spiritual concepts are beyond a child's comprehension. But many times, children are more perceptive than adults. That is one reason why Jesus invited little children to come to Him. He warned adults that they must have faith like a little child. Let's be quick to teach our children about Jesus. Then His truth will pour forth from their mouths!

Dear Lord, may I seek opportunities to instill Your truth in my children. Amen.

Poured-Out Blessings

*For I will pour water upon him that is thirsty, and floods
upon the dry ground: I will pour my spirit upon thy seed,
and my blessing upon thine offspring.*

ISAIAH 44:3 KJV

What is more refreshing than a cold glass of water after vigorous exercise or hard work? Yet how often do we see that simple glass of water as a blessing from God? What about the shade tree under which we relax? When we teach our children to say "bird" or "bunny," do we acknowledge those creatures as delightful gifts from God?

God's blessings surround us. We wonder why God isn't at work or doing more for us when in reality, He is busy right before our eyes. We're just too distracted to notice. God meets our families' needs daily, and His gifts are wonderful. Let's teach our children to recognize and praise God's goodness. Perhaps as we do this, the scales will be lifted from our own eyes, and we will begin to see God's bounty for what it really is.

---

*Dear God, Your blessings abound, but sometimes
my eyes are closed to them. Help me to see
Your great gifts that surround me. Amen.*

Be Real

We all stumble in many ways.

JAMES 3:2 NIV

Let's stop pretending. We are not "super moms." Although we put on a great facade, many days the juggling act quickly turns disastrous. It happens to everyone. You are not alone, so why fake it? Motherhood is difficult, exhausting, and overwhelming at times. We need to be real with one another. We need encouragement.

Our identity must be found in Christ alone. It cannot come from our children, husband, friends, or career. When we desire the approval of others, we have to pretend to be something we're not. The Lord knows, accepts, and loves us just as we are: imperfect. When we embrace that truth, we can be ourselves before Him and feel safe in His love. Then we are free to be real with others. Sensing a safe environment, they in turn open up to us. We have given them the freedom to be real. Mutual encouragement results when we pass on Christ's acceptance. Everyone is blessed when we are real.

Dear Lord, Your love is truly amazing. Help me grasp the unconditional love You have for me so that my relationships with others can be real. Amen.

Don't Cry Over Spilled "Stuff"

Set your affection on things above,
not on things on the earth.

COLOSSIANS 3:2 KJV

A little boy looked up at his mommy with horror on his face. He had toddled over to a chair, climbed onto it, and pulled on a shelf that contained all of Mommy's pretty things. The shelf came tumbling down on top of him. He looked at his mom, not out of pain, but fear. His wise mom realized that he was afraid he had disappointed her.

Even though she wanted him to learn safety and obedience, it was more important in that moment that she teach him that her love for him was far greater than any earthly thing she owned.

We all disobey our Father at times, putting earthly things ahead of the things above. Disobedience stems from a lack of trust in God's promises. When we fully trust that what He says is true, obedience is natural. But when we do disobey, He is swift to teach us of our wrongdoing, after we are assured of His love.

Heavenly Father, thank You for Your deep love for
me and for constantly reassuring me of it. Amen.

Leapfrog

This makes for harmony among the members,
so that all the members care for each other.
1 CORINTHIANS 12:25 NLT

On all fours, one child trustingly waits. At full speed, another child runs toward him, plants both hands on the first child's tense little back, catapults over his head, and immediately takes the waiting position on all fours. The cycle repeats itself as the children travel forward together.

In the game of leapfrog, there is no hierarchy of pride that says, "I'm better than that, so I won't do that part." If any one child refused to take his turn, the game would end.

The body of Christ is designed in exactly the same way. We each have a role, but we cannot play it alone. We all must take our turns at supporting each other and at receiving support for ourselves. God designed it this way so that we would be one in purpose, one in Him.

Father God, You have perfectly designed Your body
to function as a unit in service to You. Please grant
me the grace I need to share with others and
support them on this journey. Amen.

Abba Father

For ye have not received the spirit of bondage
again to fear; but ye have received the Spirit
of adoption, whereby we cry, Abba, Father.
ROMANS 8:15 KJV

How many times have you taken your child to day care or even Sunday school just to have her cling to your skirt? The fear of being left is almost more than she can bear. With all of your heart you want to go back, gather her in your arms, and take her with you. As she calls out, "Mommy! Mommy!" you bend down to give her one last reassuring hug.

You think about all that she will face in life and realize she'll encounter situations that are far more frightening than day care. You can help prepare her for these scary times, though. God is capable of alleviating the fears she'll face. He may not eliminate the situation, but if she trusts in Him, she will go through trials with confidence. Expose her to Christ's love while she is small. Set the example of trusting God completely.

Abba Father, how wonderful to have such a
closeness to You! Thank You for comforting me
and my children during frightening times. Amen.

Peace

For he himself is our peace.
EPHESIANS 2:14 NIV

Young children are prone to nightmares. Their active imaginations combined with their limited knowledge can create fear and anxiety. The sound of snoring becomes a roaring lion. Shadows turn into monsters. Although we may easily dismiss their fears, from our child's perspective they're legitimate. As we lay down beside them in bed, they feel secure, protected. Our presence imparts peace.

Because we have limited knowledge and understanding compared to God, we can become frightened and anxious like our children. Although God must marvel at our concerns, He knows we perceive them as real. Our husband's layoff is frightening even though God sees the new job awaiting him. We're anxious about our son's lack of control, yet God sees the mature adult he will become.

Jesus is called the Prince of Peace. His presence brings peace to our hearts. When fearful thoughts and frightening circumstances overwhelm you, trust that the Lord is right beside you. Let His words comfort your heart. May His presence impart peace.

Dear Lord, help me remember that You are always with me so that Your presence may impart peace. Amen.

Patient Encouragement

"It was I who taught Ephraim to walk, taking them by the arms. . . I led them with cords of human kindness, with ties of love. To them I was like one who lifts a little child to the cheek, and I bent down to feed them."

HOSEA 11:3-4 NIV

Teaching a young child a new skill takes love, patience, and a positive attitude. The toddler can become discouraged as he tries to fold his clothes, make his bed, or even learn to use a spoon to feed himself. Each new experience is a chance to encourage our child.

When he makes a mistake, we can make the difference in his learning experience. As mothers we demonstrate our love by encouraging him to try again, helping our child blossom to his full potential.

When we become Christians, God is the One who teaches us to be like Him. When we make a mistake, He pulls us to Him and holds us close. He uses affection to urge us to try again. His love and patience toward us are beyond expression.

God, thank You for Your example of how I should be with my child. Thank You for Your love and care for me. Amen.

The Sting

O death, where is thy sting?
O grave, where is thy victory?
1 CORINTHIANS 15:55 KJV

An excited family was traveling down the road on vacation. Suddenly, a yellow jacket flew in through a rolled-down car window! Immediately, the children started screaming hysterically. The father quickly reached up and caught the bee in his fist. After a few seconds he let it go and exclaimed, "Children, you don't have to worry now. The bee has stung me. Now it can never sting again."

What a beautiful picture of Jesus' willingness to die on the cross. He suffered the sting of death on our behalf and rose from the grave so that we might receive the gift of eternal life. Physical death no longer represents the end, but the beginning.

Many situations can frighten us: a sick child, a job loss, or marital stress. Yet the Lord does not want us to panic, for He has overcome our greatest fear—death. He can handle anything that confronts us. That truth should bring peace to our souls. Remember, there is no more sting.

Dear Lord, please forgive me when I panic.
Help me remember to trust You. Amen.

Identity Crisis

Among whom you also are the called of Jesus Christ.
ROMANS 1:6 NASB

Identity can be an ever-evolving thing. Most women, at one time in their lives, have been a daughter, sister, friend, wife, and, sometimes, all of those things at once. When those women have children, they also become Mom: cook, housekeeper, diaper changer, etc.

Your true personal identity, though, is none of those things. You are the called of Jesus Christ. You have been set apart and called by Him into the family of God. You are His child. There are no life circumstances that will alter that identity and no way that any amount of years will cause it to fade.

Begin to see yourself as He sees you. It will make your purpose so much clearer, and your roles will take on a new meaning. There need not be grief as one stage of life moves into the next, nor should there be longing for the next stage or regret over times of the past. Your true identity will never change.

Jesus, thank You for calling out to me and making me Your own. Help me to realize my true identity in You. Amen.

Choosing Words Carefully

*Let your conversation be always full of grace, seasoned with
salt, so that you may know how to answer everyone.*

COLOSSIANS 4:6 NIV

Some days, as a result of endless chatter and the many "why?"
questions, exasperation can set in. At times, it's easy for a
mom to tune out the prattle, opting to focus on her task at
hand. But conversation with our youngsters is vital for their
mental, emotional, and spiritual development.

Not only do kids learn by talking, but by listening to the
words spoken around them. The influence of those words can
gladden or grieve young hearts and spirits.

The Bible instructs us to "be pleasant" as we speak and
to "choose [our] words carefully" (Colossians 4:6). In the
everyday routine, as well as during times of godly teaching,
select words that will build up your little one. This practice is
not only for their encouragement, but also for their training
in how God desires that they speak to others. Your words can
carry God's message to their little ears!

---

*Lord Jesus, please control my tongue as I speak today.
Let my words be ones that would please
You and build my child up. Amen.*

Good Grocery Store Behavior

But thou, O Lord, art a shield for me;
my glory, and the lifter up of mine head.
PSALM 3:3 KJV

Andrea checked her grocery list. So far three-year-old Clinton had only bumped Andrea's ankles three times as he "helped" push the grocery cart. Baby Lauren cooed at smiling passersby. Andrea proudly grinned. Her beautiful little ones could have graced a magazine cover.

Until Clinton spotted a "big boy" gun in a display. When Andrea told him no, he couldn't have that toy, her model child threw a fit. Lauren began a nonstop wail. Andrea felt other shoppers' glares as she tried to quiet her children. She wanted to leave, but began grabbing formula, diapers, and other dire necessities instead.

Lord, please help me!

Peace settled over Andrea like a warm blanket. Although her children still fussed, she held her head high as she pushed her cart toward the checkout. Others may not have realized she was doing the best she could, but Jesus knew.

O Lord, I'm so glad You welcome all Your children,
even when we're not at our best. When others don't behave
well, teach me to show them the same kindness. Amen.

Teach the Word

*Set your hearts unto all the words which I testify
among you this day, which ye shall command your
children to observe to do, all the words of this law.*

DEUTERONOMY 32:46 KJV

How often do you sit back and watch as your child absorbs everything in the world around her? She is curious and excited about the things she is learning. That is why it is so important to begin sharing God's Word with her. She is not too young to be introduced to Bible stories and songs. She is even able to begin memorizing short passages of scripture.

It's more than a head knowledge, though. God not only expects you to teach your child what the Bible says, He also expects you and your child to live by it. Make a daily effort to set a godly example and to biblically train your child.

---

*Wise God, help me to use Your Word to prepare
my child for trials she will face. We want to
learn and live by Your truths. Amen.*

A Joyful Harvest

They that sow in tears shall reap in joy.
PSALM 126:5 KJV

The home is a greenhouse; the mother, a gardener.

Like a good gardener, a mother prepares the home soil with encouragement, compassion, and good home cooking so that each of her plants will grow strong and true.

She guards her plants, praying always for their protection from weeds that threaten to choke life from them. Some flourish with little effort, while others need more attention. She sweats and cries over them, praying always that the Master Gardener will water them with wisdom and truth.

Often when He does intervene, the mother-gardener is tried. Her vines may be pruned or her seedlings transplanted. Sometimes He'll allow weeds to grow, and it's all she can do to keep her hands away, to stay out of the marvelous work that He is doing.

But she trusts the hand of the Master Gardener.

And waits for a joyful harvest.

Father, thank You for the tender plants You have given me to nurture. Sometimes the gardening is hard work, but remind me that You will always return that investment with a joyful harvest. Amen.

Joy in God's Word

Thy words were found, and I did eat them; and thy
word was unto me the joy and rejoicing of mine heart:
for I am called by thy name, O LORD God of hosts.
JEREMIAH 15:16 KJV

Children have amazing ears. You might think that you can sneak a snack without their knowledge, but no matter where the children are in the house, if you open the cupboard for a piece of candy or a few chips, they will come running. You must share or risk becoming the "mean mommy."

While you might wish to hoard that last brownie, you ought to always share God's Word with your children. When you are excited about a truth you find in scripture, your children will pick up on that. They will learn that God's Word is the sweetest pleasure they will ever enjoy. Maybe as you share a snack of cookies and milk, you can learn a verse together. What a wonderful way to share God's Word with your little ones!

Father, Your Word is delightful. Help my
children and me to savor it together. Amen.

Blind Trust

And thine ears shall hear a word behind thee,
saying, This is the way, walk ye in it.
ISAIAH 30:21 KJV

Toddlers have a mind of their own. They can have every intention of going in the direction their mother tells them, but the instant they see something interesting, all other intentions are lost in the desire to investigate. This takes a multitude of patience on the mother's part. We have to be willing to repeat our directions and hope that our child will learn to listen.

God is always with us, giving us directions on which path to follow. The lure of the world can entice us to take an excursion along a route that is different than the one God has for us. When this happens, we can be in danger, physically and spiritually. We must train our ear to hear God's voice. He doesn't shout directions. When we are still and quiet, listening for Him, we will hear the way He has for us. We no longer have to fret about anything, but can rest in His decisions.

Thank You, Lord, for caring about every step I take.
Please help me to hear You. Amen.

He who began a good work in you will carry it
on to completion until the day of Christ Jesus.
PHILIPPIANS 1:6 NIV

Jenny didn't feel she had adequate Bible knowledge to be able to teach her young child the Bible. There were even times in raising her child that she had questions about what to do. She desired people with whom she could discuss her child-rearing ideas.

God promises that He will complete the work of growing us spiritually. When we accepted the Lord Jesus as our personal Savior (John 3:16), the Holy Spirit began to live in us. That Holy Spirit empowers us to understand what God is teaching us as He matures us spiritually (John 14:26). Our Christian walk is a process of growing into the image of Christ. Joining a Bible study for moms, taking a parenting class, and reading Christian books on child-rearing—all will assist us in growing spiritually and as mothers. Rest assured, God will complete the good work that He has begun in us.

Lord, lead me to the Christ-centered resources
You provide in growing me spiritually and as a
mother to raise my child for Your glory. Amen.

Thankful for God's Wisdom

I thank thee, and praise thee, O thou God of my fathers,
who hast given me wisdom and might, and hast made
known unto me now what we desired of thee.

DANIEL 2:23 KJV

Angela and Valerie were enjoying a visit over a cup of coffee. As they reminisced about their college days, their children shared a playdate nearby.

"You know, Val, it's amazing the new perspective a person has on life once she has children," Angela commented. "When I was in college, it seemed like I was the only one affected by my decisions. Back then I thought I had some tough decisions to make, but now every choice impacts the lives of my husband and son."

Valerie nodded. "I know what you mean. Suddenly life requires more responsibility. I want only the best for Adeline, but I don't always know what that is. God's wisdom has never failed me, though. Some decisions aren't easy, because what He wants is sometimes different than what my family and friends want, but He shows me what's right."

Thank You, God, for giving me the strength and wisdom
to do what's right even when I face adversity. Amen.

Blessed Rest

Then God. . .rested from all His work.

GENESIS 2:3 NASB

The schedule of a mommy is so full, typically without a moment to spare. The day begins with getting your child dressed and fed and doesn't slow down until you wearily drop into your bed after getting them tucked in. It's then that you realize that you can't remember when you last had "me time."

Think of something that you enjoy that could bring some refreshment to your wearied body—then do it! Take a few moments to read. . .even if it's just one article from your favorite magazine. Or relax for a few minutes while you listen to your favorite music. Just those few brief moments can be revitalizing!

This isn't time meant to compile your list of things to do tomorrow. This is time set aside just for you. Remember, God has set the example of rest after work. . .and if He did it, it must be a practice that has merit!

Dear God, remind me to take the time to rest, just as You did, so that I can be the mommy You want me to be. Amen.

Reflecting God

For the message of the cross is foolishness to those who are perishing, but to us who are being saved it is the power of God.

1 CORINTHIANS 1:18 NKJV

As the mother pushed the cart through the huge warehouse store, searching for the items she needed, her young daughter sat in the basket. Becoming bored, the child began to sing. The mother could tell she was singing songs she'd learned in Sunday school. Some passersby smiled at the boisterous songs, while others grumbled about the noise.

When we are enamored with God, we shouldn't hide the joy we have in our relationship with Him. Our exuberance reflects the character of God to a darkened world around us. Even in times of trouble, we should be filled with a peace and quiet joy that makes the world wonder what we have that is different.

Some people will understand our joy; others might grumble at our ability to find delight in the midst of adversity. We must reflect God, no matter the outlook of those around us.

Lord, help me to be joyful in my relationship with You. Amen.

The Source of Real Strength

My soul melteth for heaviness: strengthen
thou me according unto thy word.

PSALM 119:28 KJV

Being a mother is the toughest job you'll ever have, but a Christian mother gathers her strength from the Word of God. Yet when the going gets tough, our time in the Word is often the first thing that goes.

Instead of running to the Father in a crisis, we turn to others for comfort and are hurt when they fail us. Instead of crying out to the Lord for help, we try to pull ourselves out of pits we have dug until we are exhausted.

Spurred on by the same mentality that affects our children, we stomp our feet and say, "I can do it by myself!" But we know we cannot.

Fortunately, our patient Father loves us too much to allow us to stay in this sorry state. He will lovingly orchestrate circumstances to bring us back to Himself and to His Word.

And there we will find wisdom and comfort and strength.

O God, my strength, when I begin neglecting
Your Word, lovingly pull me back to it,
for it is the true source of strength. Amen.

Don't Run with Scissors

The proverbs of Solomon the son of David,
king of Israel; To know wisdom and instruction;
to perceive the words of understanding.

PROVERBS 1:1-2 KJV

Don't run with scissors, don't play with fire, and don't throw a ball in the house. Those are all pieces of motherly wisdom that have been handed down through the generations. The book of Proverbs is referred to as the book of wisdom because Solomon was endowed with both spiritual and practical wisdom from God. Wisdom is being able to discern the things that produce good results and also understanding what causes negative results. But wisdom is just the first step.

We notice in Proverbs 1:2, that wisdom is linked with instruction. We can pray for wisdom, and we can search the scriptures for knowledge, but without action, our knowledge means nothing. It's not the knowledge that's key, it's the application of that knowledge. So, if we are to truly be wise, we should not only know but act upon the will of God.

Jesus, please give me a dose of Your wisdom and the
strength to carry it out through my actions. Amen.

Forever Safe

"I give them eternal life, and they shall never perish;
no one will snatch them out of my hand."

JOHN 10:28 NIV

A precocious three-year-old slowly approached the cage of a sleeping lion at the zoo. Suddenly, the old lion opened its mouth and let out a deafening roar! The frightened toddler turned and ran frantically in the opposite direction.

Have you ever felt like that terrified toddler? Unfortunately, Satan has a way of frightening us. He plants "what-if" thoughts in our mind that evoke fear. He speaks condemning words to our heart. Yet we must realize that all Satan can do is frighten us. He has no power over us. He cannot pluck us from God's hand.

The toddler reacted out of fear, not realizing that she was safe. The lion was contained behind bars. We must grasp spiritual truth. Although Satan may scare us, we are eternally safe because Jesus has defeated Satan. Jesus imparts that same victory to believers. Let's not be frightened, but feel safe and secure in our Father's hand.

Dear Lord, thank You for defeating Satan, and help me
remember that I am safe in Your hand. Amen.

Thank-You Note from Jesus

"And the King will answer them, 'Truly, I say to you, as you did it to one of the least of these my brothers, you did it to me.'"

MATTHEW 25:40 ESV

Every mother of a young child will agree that caring for little children can be completely draining. And usually, it's a thankless task, with no end in sight. The pile of laundry never grows smaller, the toys never stay in the toy box, there are play groups, swimming lessons, and, oh, we mustn't forget doctor's appointments and church activities. All of those things are managed by Mom, with nary a thank you.

Matthew 25:40 is a thank-you note from Jesus. He says thank you for the tears that you dry when offering His comfort, and thank you for the hugs that you give as an extension of His love. Whatever is done, in the name of Jesus Christ, for the weak ones whom He has placed in your charge, it is done for Him.

Thank You, Jesus, for the reminder that I serve You as I carry out my tasks as a mother. Please continue to use me to share Your love. Amen.

*But Jesus beheld them, and said unto them, With men
this is impossible; but with God all things are possible.*
MATTHEW 19:26 KJV

Josie twisted her hands in her lap. Megan had been standing beside her one moment and gone the next. Josie listened to the store manager talk to security on the phone, but she couldn't just wait in his office. She headed back into the store.

"Lord, I can't find her. Please protect my baby," Josie prayed as she looked under clothes racks for her precious daughter. The three-year-old had never wandered off before. Panic threatened to choke Josie. She closed her eyes and prayed. The urge to go to the bedding department pulled her in that direction. As she entered, she called her daughter's name.

A quiet little voice answered, "Mommy?"

Josie watched as her daughter crawled out from under a pile of fluffy pillows. She ran to her little girl, hugged her close, and praised God above for finding her baby.

---

*Lord, I would like to think that I am in control
of every situation, but I know I am not. I'm glad
You are always with me and my child. Amen.*

Teach by Example

Moreover as for me, God forbid that I should sin against the LORD in ceasing to pray for you: but I will teach you the good and the right way.

1 SAMUEL 12:23 KJV

"Now I lay me down to sleep...." How precious and promising it is to hear a young child who is learning to pray. It is precious because the sweetness of that child's heart overflows as he communicates with the heavenly Father. It is promising because it indicates that there is someone in that child's life who loves him enough to teach him the importance of prayer.

Our little ones need us to pray for them. We must choose to do right for our children both in interceding to God on their behalf and in setting a good example of what a proper prayer life should be. There are so many things our little ones need to learn. Let's make their spiritual training a priority.

Heavenly Father, help my children as they are at the beginning of life's journey. Let them learn the joy of prayer even now. Amen.

Activity Overload

"Woman, why do you involve me?"
Jesus replied. "My hour has not yet come."
JOHN 2:4 NIV

Sarah closed her car door and walked toward the other moms in the elementary school parking lot. Approaching the women, she was greeted by smiles as the conversation continued.

"We're so busy," Becky stated. "There is the homework and school activities, but the kids are also involved in community sports, dance, and music lessons. My oldest is taking up wrestling soon too."

Sarah understood the looks the other moms were giving each other. Becky pushed her kids hard. She wanted her children to excel at everything, but at what cost to the children's need for a childhood?

Jesus' mother, Mary, did a similar thing to Jesus at a wedding. She knew that her Son was the Messiah and that He had God's power. In a way, she was pushing Him to reveal His glory before His time had come. Jesus lovingly let His mother know she needed to allow Him to be who He was at that time.

Lord, help me to guide my children through
their days without being controlling. Amen.

Comfort in Prayer

If we are distressed, it is for your comfort and salvation;
if we are comforted, it is for your comfort.

2 CORINTHIANS 1:6 NIV

All children go through phases as they grow. There are times when they test the boundaries set for them, which, in turn, test a mother's patience. Some stages are so difficult we wonder if they will ever pass. The mother can feel isolated, particularly if none of her friends have had children go through the same experience.

In this situation, the best resort is prayer. God understands all we are going through. His "children" often go through periods when they don't listen to His leading. He is the parent with the most patience and the most trying children. He will help you through this time of aloneness.

When one stage passes to the next, we can breathe a sigh of relief. God allows us to be distressed so that we can encourage others in similar situations. When another mother confides in us, we can pray with her and assure her that God is there to see her through.

Lord, help me be there for other mothers
and encourage them with Your love. Amen.

Teach Me about You

*That I may know him, and the power of his
resurrection, and the fellowship of his sufferings,
being made conformable unto his death.*

PHILIPPIANS 3:10 KJV

Jessica opened her Bible and began to read where she'd left off the day before. The sound of bare feet running down the hallway reached her ears long before her three-year-old daughter rounded the corner.

"Whatcha doing?"

Jessica pulled her onto her lap. "Reading my Bible."

"Why?"

Jessica stood and carried her daughter back to her bedroom. "Because I want to know all about God, and there are a lot of things that I don't understand, so I like to read my Bible." She tucked her daughter back into bed.

"I want to learn too. Mommy, read me a story, pleeease."

Jessica picked up the children's Bible that had been sitting beside the bed. "I'll read you one story, and then you have to take your nap." Satisfied with her daughter's nod, Jessica read her the story of David and Goliath. The little girl fell asleep long before the story was complete.

---

*Father God, thank You for reminding me to
teach my child to read Your Word daily. Amen.*

A Peaceful Home

*"Blessed are the peacemakers,
for they will be called children of God."*

MATTHEW 5:9 NIV

Do you strive to live life like Jesus? Do you have a peaceful home? Are you modeling Christ, the "Prince of Peace" (Isaiah 9:6 NIV), to your child?

In the Sermon on the Mount, Jesus provided the mind and heart perspective and the avenue to be blessed, fortunate, or happy. We will be blessed by being called God's children when we are peacemakers.

What does it mean to be a peacemaker when we have a young child in the home? First, it means we have a steadfast mind, as we trust Him (Isaiah 26:3); we "set [our] minds on things above" (Colossians 3:2 NIV). Second, we invite Jesus to provide a structure that is most suitable to a peaceful home. For example, scheduled morning devotionals, mealtimes as a family, nap and rest times, playtimes. Finally, through Mom modeling a right relationship with the Lord, the result will be inner peace, quiet resting places, and a peaceful home (Isaiah 32:17–18).

Lord, please help me fix my eyes on You and model in mind, heart, and behavior the Prince of Peace. Amen.

Fellowship

*Not giving up meeting together, as some are in
the habit of doing, but encouraging one another—
and all the more as you see the Day approaching.*

HEBREWS 10:25 NIV

One Sunday a newlywed couple awoke to the sound of rain pelting their bedroom window. The wife was tempted to roll over and skip church. As a child, her mother had occasionally used the rain as an excuse to sleep in. The husband had the opposite inclination. His family always went to church on rainy Sundays because playing golf was not an option. Laughing, they decided that their family would attend church come rain or shine!

Christians need one another. Just as a burning pile of coal radiates heat and light, so fellowship with other believers fans our spiritual flames. We are encouraged, built up, and spurred on. Together we radiate God's love to a world needing the Light of Truth. God has made the church body for you, and you for the church body. We need each other. Purpose to fellowship, come rain or shine!

*Dear Lord, help me realize the importance of Christian
fellowship. I need other believers and they need me. Amen.*

Patient Love

Charity suffereth long, and is kind.
1 CORINTHIANS 13:4 KJV

Two young mothers sat together, enjoying a rare bit of quiet time. As they talked, they shared the many joys and woes of motherhood.

"I feel like such a failure," the one lamented. "No matter what I say or do, I just can't seem to get through to my daughter. After so long, I just start yelling. I know it's wrong, but I can't seem to help it."

"You're not alone," her friend replied. "We all go through it. Your prayer and patience *will* pay off. Just be sure to give your struggles to Jesus every day—even several times a day."

It was encouragement that both friends needed. Children need to know what their limits are. At times those lessons are more difficult for the mother than they are for the child. But with God's help, the battle that at first looked like a lost cause will become one of the most precious victories ever won.

Lord, I know that I must often frustrate You, but You're still lovingly molding me into Christlikeness. Help me also to show loving patience as I raise my child. Amen.

Perseverance

We also glory in our sufferings, because we know that
suffering produces perseverance; perseverance,
character; and character, hope.

ROMANS 5:3–4 NIV

Not again! It seemed more than any parents should have to bear. Their four-year-old daughter was facing her third open-heart surgery. At two days old, she had experienced the first, and another at nine months. Everyone had prayed that this third operation would not be necessary. It seemed the Lord had other plans.

How do we persevere through trials that seem unbearable? Our only hope is to turn toward God and not away from Him. Trusting the Lord in the midst of suffering is an act of obedience. It is refusing to go down the path riddled with despair, hopelessness, and anxiety. Instead, it is choosing to lean upon the Lord's strength, faithfulness, and power. He imparts inner peace in difficulties that scream despair. When we persevere, Christ's character is revealed in and through us. Hope is realized. Let's persevere in our sufferings in order to obtain the hope that God has promised.

Dear Lord, You know how difficult suffering can be.
Help me turn to You and persevere. Build my
character, and give me hope. Amen.

Whosoever will come after me, let him deny himself,
and take up his cross, and follow me.
MARK 8:34 KJV

New experiences can be frightening for a young child. Perhaps it's the first day of nursery school, a new babysitter, or simply a situation not encountered before. Often the child will want to hide behind his or her mother, unsure how to act. When we encourage our children to do something despite their misgivings, they often enjoy the experience more than they could ever have imagined.

Jesus asks us to be witnesses for Him in a multitude of ways. For some, this means to go into the mission field in a foreign country. For others, they are to reach out to those they come in contact with in everyday situations.

Often, the thought of doing this makes us uncomfortable. We don't want to step outside our comfort zone. Yet we must remember this is what Jesus asked us to do. When we follow His directive, we will be blessed beyond measure.

Thank You, Jesus, for Your encouragement. Help me
to take that step of faith and reach out to others. Amen.

Anything but That!

He said, "Take now your son, your only son, whom you love,
Isaac, and go to the land of Moriah, and offer him there as a
burnt offering on one of the mountains of which I will tell you."

GENESIS 22:2 NASB

What God asked Abraham to do was absolutely shocking. Sacrifice his promised son, whom his wife Sarah was amazingly able to have *after* her youth. The story tells us that just as Abraham was about to sacrifice Isaac, an angel of the Lord called down from heaven and told Abraham not to lay a hand on his son.

Abraham had a faith and trust in God that defies today's need for information. We want to know *who, what, where, when, how,* and especially *why.* Abraham undoubtedly wanted to know too. Still, if God told him to do something, Abraham did it.

God was trying to teach and grow Abraham. Because of this test, Abraham realized again that Isaac did not belong to him, but to God. Like Abraham, we have been entrusted by God to love and care for our children.

Lord, I give my children over to You
because You are the true Father. Amen.

Growing Up

And in Christ you have been brought to fullness.
He is the head over every power and authority.
COLOSSIANS 2:10 NIV

Jimmy worked alongside his mother in the garden. As she worked, Jimmy asked lots of questions.

"How do veshibles grow?"

She smiled at his pronunciation. "God sends rain and sunshine."

Jimmy tried to get a better grip on the neck of a yellow squash. "Does God make them grow big too?"

"Yes, He does."

"Am I a veshible in God's garden? I'm growing up too."

She laughed. "Well, you aren't a vegetable, but you are one of God's children."

"Daddy says we are blessed to have this garden. Is that right?"

She thought of all the food that she'd put away for the winter. It was tiring work, but it was also a blessing. Her husband worked in construction, and sometimes the weather limited his working hours. During those times, the home-canned goods would feed them when there was no money for groceries. "Yes, we are very blessed, Jimmy."

Thank You, Lord, for filling my life with love and supplying all our needs. Thank You for providing for my family. Amen.

Lying Down

He maketh me to lie down in green pastures:
he leadeth me beside the still waters.

PSALM 23:2 KJV

Do you ever wonder why your child fights you when it's nap time? You try desperately to get him into his bed for some much-needed rest. As you struggle, you think, *Why is this child refusing this wonderful opportunity? No one would have to tell me twice to take a nap!*

Why is it then that our Shepherd has to make us lie down in green pastures? It might be true that we would like to rest a few moments here or there, but there are just so many things to be accomplished.

Pushing hard isn't always in our best interest, though. Consider this: God rested; Jesus rested, and He commanded His disciples to rest too. Why is it that we mothers feel we are exempt from this need? For our sakes and our family's sake we must take a break so that we are refreshed. Why not allow yourself this much-needed pleasure today?

Dear Shepherd, You've shown me that I do need
rest to function properly. Help me to find
time and not be stubborn about it. Amen.

Guarding Our Children's Hearts

Above all else, guard your heart,
for everything you do flows from it.
PROVERBS 4:23 NIV

The Lord tells us that, above all else, we need to guard our hearts because from them flows the wellspring of life. Our children do not know how to guard their hearts. Therefore, the responsibility resides with us as their mothers to guard their hearts until they are mature enough to do it for themselves. How do we guard their hearts? We need to be diligent in not allowing anything of the "world" to permeate their lives. That means we guard with vigilance what our children are exposed to in regard to TV, internet, friends, books, and magazines. It also means we focus on what we do want our children to be exposed to, such as the Bible, church, Sunday school, or other children raised with the same Christ-centered purpose we have.

Lord, direct me to guard my children's hearts from
all that is contrary to a Christ-centered purpose,
and guide me to expose my children's hearts to all
that is in line with Your purpose. Amen.

Faith Demonstrated

*Since they could not get him to Jesus because of the crowd,
they made an opening in the roof above Jesus by digging
through it and then lowered the mat the man was lying on.*

MARK 2:4 NIV

The men were desperate and undeterred! Their friend was paralyzed, and Jesus was preaching at a house in Capernaum. When the crowded room would not accommodate the paralytic's stretcher, they hoisted him to the roof. After digging a hole, they lowered him inside the house through the opening. Jesus was moved by their faith and healed their paralyzed friend.

What are we willing to sacrifice to bring our friends before Jesus? To what extent are we willing to be inconvenienced?

Like the paralytic's friends, we, too, must believe that Jesus is the answer. Our faith will then compel us to lay our friends before the Lord in prayer. Let's put our faith into action by diligently placing our family and friends before the Lord in prayer. The Lord will faithfully answer.

---

*Lord, may I demonstrate my faith in You by
diligently praying for others. Give me strength
and determination to persevere. Amen.*

Me? Homeschool?

For I know the thoughts that I think toward you,
saith the LORD, thoughts of peace, and not of evil,
to give you an expected end.
JEREMIAH 29:11 KJV

"Thank you for coming in, Mrs. Pope." The twins' teacher walked around her massive desk.

Mary sat up straighter in her chair. "You're welcome."

"I expect that you know why I've asked you here?"

"What have the twins done now?" Mary asked, feeling herself slip down into the cushions of the chair as Mrs. Pope began reading off her list of grievances against the children.

Later, as she drove the children home, Mary prayed. She wanted what was best for the twins but felt that public schools were not the answer. The thought that she could homeschool them entered her thoughts. Would she be able to do the job right and teach the children what they needed to succeed in life? She felt the Lord's urging and knew deep in her heart that she could.

Please be with me, Lord, as I strive to make the right decisions
where my children are concerned, and continue to allow
Your peace to reside in me. In Jesus' name, amen.

Making Cookies with God

For we are His workmanship, created in Christ Jesus
for good works, which God prepared beforehand
that we should walk in them.
EPHESIANS 2:10 NKJV

"I want to help!" Children are notorious for turning a simple job, like making cookies, into an unbelievable mess. Inevitably, there will be flour sprinkled on everything, eggshells in the batter, extra dishes to wash, and a chocolate-covered face to scrub upon completion of the task.

Of course, the task would be accomplished so much faster and more neatly if Mom just waited and did it by herself during her child's nap time. But then her child would miss out on the experience of working toward an accomplishment, along with the joy of working with Mommy.

So it is with our heavenly Father. He could accomplish His will with much greater effectiveness and efficiency without our help. Yet He chooses to use us to help Him carry out His plans. He simply smiles when we feel like we have done well, and He waits until we aren't looking to pick out the eggshells.

Father, help me to be as patient and understanding
with my child as You are with me. Amen.

Refreshment

Therefore my heart is glad, and my glory rejoiceth:
my flesh also shall rest in hope.

PSALM 16:9 KJV

Do you ever feel pulled in a dozen different ways? Before your eyes open in the morning, one of the children is crying or calling for you. Someone in your family asks you a favor. The church wants you to help with a program. A friend calls for advice. By the end of the day when you finally crawl into bed, you are exhausted. In the midst of caring for little ones and doing what you can for others, you've had no time for God. Guilt rears up, because you know spending time with God is the most important part of every day.

God never makes demands on us. He is always there waiting for us. God understands the necessities of our daily lives. When we fall into bed at the end of the day, we have the opportunity to take a few moments of spiritual refreshment with God, to relax into His rest, knowing there will come a day when we'll have more time with Him.

O God, make my heart glad because You
are patient and understanding. Amen.

My God Knows

*Your Father knoweth what things
ye have need of, before ye ask him.*

MATTHEW 6:8 KJV

How are you when it comes to asking for help? It's true that all mothers have different personalities, but in general we want to be self-sufficient. We don't like to admit it when we are completely worn out, when we barely have time to pick up our children's toys or make a decent meal. We want to appear competent, so we just keep quiet.

We might burn ourselves out fooling those around us, but we can't fool God. He knows what our needs are before we even share them with Him. He wants to help us, but we have to want His help. Why not willingly give your needs and concerns to your heavenly Father, who loves you and wants so much to help you? It will relieve a tremendous amount of pressure and bring much joy to your home. Swallow your pride. It's a foe that almost always defeats, but God will give you the victory.

---

*Father, I'm sorry I've tried to hide my concerns
from You. I place them in Your hands today,
knowing You'll care for me. Amen.*

Will They Ever Grow Up?

*And the child Samuel grew on, and was in
favour both with the LORD, and also with men.*
1 SAMUEL 2:26 KJV

We spend our days cleaning up spilled milk, being interrupted when providing instruction, and breaking up fights over toys. Some days we wonder, *Will they ever grow up?*

Oh, yes, they will grow up.

They will get bigger, stronger, more coordinated. They will learn to talk and, eventually, to converse. And they will learn to think for themselves.

If we want our children to be like Samuel, growing in favor with God and men, we need to be as patient with our little ones as God is with us. We need to speak to them firmly but gently, encouraging them as they grow and steering them in the right direction. Kids will be kids, so we shouldn't be surprised when they act like kids. They will all too soon grow up, and we'll be wishing they were little again. In the meantime, be patient.

After all, there's no use crying over spilled milk.

*Father, thank You for being patient with me;
help me be patient with my little ones. Amen.*

Your Body, God's Temple

Do you not know that your bodies are temples of the Holy Spirit, who is in you, whom you have received from God?

1 CORINTHIANS 6:19 NIV

Many moms, when viewing themselves in the mirror, can quickly count up multiple changes they would like to make. Maybe the hairstyle is out of date, or a few pounds should be shed, or those laugh lines aren't really so funny. It's amazing how quickly the imperfections can be spotted and criticized.

It is essential to keep our bodies healthy for our own well-being as well as for the sake of our children, but that should not be where we invest all of our time and effort. After inviting Christ to live in your heart, your body becomes His home, a temple where the Holy Spirit lives (1 Corinthians 6:19). God does not require that our bodies be ones of perfection; however, out of a heart of love for Him, we should choose to maintain His temple to the best of our ability.

Father, help me to accept myself today as a woman created by You for the purpose of housing Your Holy Spirit. Amen.

How Far?

For as the heaven is high above the earth, so great is his mercy toward them that fear him. As far as the east is from the west, so far hath he removed our transgressions from us.

PSALM 103:11-12 KJV

After days of clouds and rain, we mothers breathe a sigh of relief and take our kids to the park. Most of us do not think about the source of our bright, lovely weather—the sun, our closest star, located 93 million miles from Earth.

Facts and figures about the stars may fascinate astronomers and astronauts, but we must focus attention on our little balls of fire that zoom past us like miniature meteors. Who has time to ponder how far the east is from the west? What was the psalmist talking about when he wrote in such poetic, cosmic language long ago?

Just this: Jesus went out of His way—much farther than 93 million miles—to sacrifice His holy life for us. His love is so high it can never be measured.

Lord Jesus, thank You for the poets of the psalms, who help me understand the vastness of Your love a little better. Amen.

No Place for Envy

Let us not be desirous of vain glory,
provoking one another, envying one another.
GALATIANS 5:26 KJV

You want to be a good mother. Maybe you even promised God that if He would give you a child, you would be "the perfect parent." Now you find yourself in a grocery store checkout line. Your sweet little angel is showing a rather wild side as he crawls over the cart, pulls gum and magazines from the rack, and screams when you deny his request for a treat. You catch a glimpse of the children in the next aisle. They are standing quietly in their proper places, and you begin to think, *Why is my child so difficult and that woman's kids so perfect?* You resent the "perfect" mom because her "perfect" kids are making you look bad.

Take a deep breath. Remember that all kids are different, as are moms. You have strengths that other moms only dream about. Your little one was designed by God especially for you. Teach him well, and love him always.

Dear God, sometimes I'm jealous of other
moms' abilities. Forgive me, and help me
to be a mother who honors You. Amen.

Future Saints

I will pour out my spirit upon all flesh;
and your sons and your daughters shall prophesy.
JOEL 2:28 KJV

What a hot afternoon! Sarah was glad she had bought a wading pool for the twins' birthday. It created a nice, cool break before the kids' naps. Three-year-old Callie and Carter played happily with their new water toys. But Sarah soon found herself separating screeching children. She tried to calm them, but they nearly yanked her arms off as they fought like little tiger cubs. Sarah even tried to pray, but she feared the twins would kill each other before the amen.

It never failed. Whenever Sarah attempted to grow spiritually, her kids always turned into little heathens. *Lord, what will they be like when they're teenagers?* She shuddered. But Sarah decided to keep trying.

Fourteen years later, Callie and Carter were singing in a Christian band. Several other teens came to hear the music, and they helped lead others their age to Christ.

Father, in the daily war to survive, help me never underestimate what You do by Your Spirit in my children's lives. Thank You for making me part of the miracle. Amen.

Tough Love

Do everything in love.
1 CORINTHIANS 16:14 NIV

Paula pulled her child's bedroom door shut behind her. His sobs pierced her heart. It would be so easy to go back into the bedroom, pull him into her arms, and simply love on him. But she knew that if she did, he wouldn't learn the lesson she was trying to teach him.

Instead, she prayed. Tears streamed down her face as she visited with the Lord about her little boy's refusal to obey the simple rules she'd put into place. As she sat quietly, Paula realized her actions were correct and true.

Tough love had to be administered now while her baby was still young. Paula knew she wanted him to grow up to be a godly man. She tiptoed to his room. He'd cried himself to sleep. Paula kissed his forehead and heard his soft whisper, "I love you, Mommy."

"I love you too, pumpkin," she whispered back, thankful she hadn't caved earlier but had taken her feelings to the Lord.

Father, I know that I need You to help me when I have to use tough love and then stand my ground. I love You, Lord. Amen.

One Thing

One thing I have desired of the LORD, that will I seek: That I may dwell in the house of the LORD all the days of my life, to behold the beauty of the LORD, and to inquire in His temple.

PSALM 27:4 NKJV

Consider Mary and Martha. Jesus said, "Martha, Martha. . . you are worried and upset about many things, but few things are needed—or indeed only *one*. Mary has chosen what is better, and it will not be taken away from her" (Luke 10:41-42 NIV, emphasis added). Martha allowed the urgent things that arose in her day to crowd out the one important thing: time with her Savior.

As moms, we could all make a list of the urgent things that need to get done each day. But knowing that our children need us to be the best that we can be, and that we can only achieve that through a right relationship with God, we need to set aside the urgent things in order to make time for the *one thing* first—time with our Father—the most important thing in our day.

Father, help me to dedicate more time to simply being with You. Amen.

A Peaceful Life

"Peace I leave with you; my peace I give you.
I do not give to you as the world gives. Do not
let your hearts be troubled and do not be afraid."

JOHN 14:27 NIV

We know that in this life, there will be conflict, stress, worries, and disobedient children. However, in the challenges of raising children, Jesus has left us with—and desires to continually give us—peace. The stipulation is that the type of peace the world gives—the temporal, brief, counterfeit peace— is not God's eternal peace. When we believe in our hearts and confess with our lips that Jesus is Lord, we are saved (Romans 10:9). As believers we have Jesus' Spirit (John 15:5), the Holy Spirit (John 14:26), the Prince of Peace (Isaiah 9:6) indwelling us. With the eternal security of being at peace with the Lord and peace indwelling us, we are then free to "not be anxious about anything, but in every situation, by prayer and petition, with thanksgiving, present [our] requests to God" (Philippians 4:6 NIV).

Lord, thank You for Your peace that surpasses
all understanding, and is given to me so I
can live a peaceful life. Amen.

Stuff

*"Do not store up for yourselves treasures on earth,
where moths and vermin destroy, and where thieves
break in and steal. But store up for yourselves treasures
in heaven, where moths and vermin do not destroy,
and where thieves do not break in and steal."*

MATTHEW 6:19–20 NIV

Jesus reminds us that everything we see is temporary. None of our earthly possessions will enter heaven's gates. Then why do we spend so much time, money, and energy obtaining temporary treasures? Jesus encourages us to concentrate on eternal treasures instead. Spending time studying God's Word and growing closer to Him is a wise investment. Pouring our lives into people reaps lasting benefits. Using material blessings to spiritually impact others is commended.

Rather than storing up "stuff," let's pass it on so that others may be blessed. Focus on things that will last forever and never lose their value. When we store up heavenly treasures, we will be blessed in this life and the life to come.

*Dear Lord, help me focus on heavenly rather
than earthly treasures. Open my eyes to
see life from Your perspective. Amen.*

Under Construction

Rejoice always, pray continually, give thanks in all circumstances; for this is God's will for you in Christ Jesus.
1 THESSALONIANS 5:16-18 NIV

Surely, when God said to give thanks for everything, He didn't mean the time when the baby had the flu and shared the virus with the entire family. Or when we had to scrub an unidentifiable stickiness off the carpet.

But God didn't qualify His biblical admonishment of giving thanks in all things; He really meant every circumstance in our life—annoying, frustrating, even ordinary moments. He promises to never leave or forsake us, even in the middle of the night when the baby has a dirty diaper. Or while we're scraping off a half-eaten Pop-Tart from the car seat.

Giving thanks reminds us that what really matters is that God is at work in us. Our patience is growing, our kindness is stretching, and our love is being made perfect. At all times, we're in process and under construction.

Lord, thank You for continuing to do Your good work in me and in my children. Amen.

Happy Are Those Who Endure

*Behold, we count them happy which endure. Ye have heard
of the patience of Job, and have seen the end of the Lord;
that the Lord is very pitiful, and of tender mercy.*

JAMES 5:11 KJV

Alone with her baby in a newborn intensive care unit, the tired
mother kept vigil. She stayed by her baby's side, watching
monitors, wrestling with tubing and cables as she tried to
nurse, asking God to see her through this crisis.

She watched the other parents in the nursery as they
labored over their infants, most of whom had been born pre-
maturely. Each weight check came with anxiety; each ounce
gained brought hope.

With each discharge, there was great joy on the ward, the
parents and staff rejoicing when a baby was big enough to
leave. They all shared the success, because they had all known
the struggle.

Happy were those who endured.

---

*Father, in an hour of crisis, I readily seek Your mercy and
strength to endure. But in the daily routine of motherhood,
I sometimes forget that You are there to sustain me. Thank
You for being with me through thick and thin. Amen.*

Resting and Waiting

Rest in the LORD, and wait patiently for him: fret not thyself because of him who prospereth in his way, because of the man who bringeth wicked devices to pass.

PSALM 37:7 KJV

There was a tug at the blanket. "Mama, it's light outside, and I'm hungry," three-year-old Megan stated firmly. Erin groaned as she looked at the clock. 7:30.

Another sleepless night filled with nothing but worry, Erin thought dejectedly. It seemed like her life was completely consumed by fear. *What if I don't raise Megan right? If something happens to me, what will become of her?* The more Erin worried, the more sleep she lost. The more sleep she lost, the more she worried. It was a horrible cycle that she couldn't break.

Finally, she talked to her pastor's wife. "Erin, there are many things beyond our control, but they aren't beyond God's control," the wise lady reminded her. "You need to let Him manage your fears."

As Erin prayed, her burden began to lift. That night, her rest was sweet.

Dear God, many times I am fearful, and rest evades me. I now cast my cares on You, for You will see me through. Amen.

Treasured Moments

I will greatly rejoice in the LORD, my soul shall be joyful in my God; for he hath clothed me with the garments of salvation, he hath covered me with the robe of righteousness.

ISAIAH 61:10 KJV

Have you ever watched your child and been struck by the depth of love you have for him? This is a love so intense it is almost a physical ache. At that moment you may want nothing other than to spend more time with your toddler, watching and getting to know him as he grows. We can stand in wonder as we watch our offspring learn new skills or discover the world around them. We thrill over first hugs or kisses, never getting enough and thankful for each one bestowed.

When we stop to contemplate the gifts God has given us—salvation, love, grace, mercy—we are filled with incredible wonder. We can rejoice, knowing that God will always delight in us as much as we delight in Him. He, too, is thankful for each expression of love we extend to Him.

Thank You, God, for Your indescribable gift through Your Son, Jesus Christ, and for Your love for me. Amen.

Source of Strength

I love you, LORD, my strength.
PSALM 18:1 NIV

God's Word tells us repeatedly that He is our source of strength (1 Chronicles 29:12; Psalm 68:35; Colossians 1:11). Sometimes in our weary and exhausted state, God calls us to wait on Him, promising that those who wait will renew their strength (Isaiah 40:29-31). As we rely on God's supernatural strength, He does provide mothers with practical tips on how to survive life: prayer, walking in close union with the Lord (John 15:5), trusting and allowing the Lord to prioritize our commitments, saying no to what is not God's will, taking naps when our children nap or have quiet playtime in their rooms, going to bed thirty minutes earlier at night, staying organized, and making meals over the weekend that will provide leftovers for several nights. As an exhausted mother, take hope. The Lord, our source of strength, will empower us to accomplish all things in His will (Philippians 4:13).

Lord, I thank You for being my source of strength and hope.
I praise You that I can raise my child and complete
the work You have for me in Your power. Amen.

Speak, Lord!

So Eli told Samuel, "Go and lie down, and if he calls you,
say, 'Speak, LORD, for your servant is listening.' "

1 SAMUEL 3:9 NIV

God may not speak audibly to us today, but He does speak. He
speaks clearly through His Word. Nature declares His praise.
Other people communicate God's truth. Circumstances can
confirm His will. Are we listening?

Today's women are bombarded by voices that emphasize
having perfect children, Martha Stewart homes, and youthful
bodies. We strain to hear God's voice whispering truth amid
the clamor. What is the solution? We must purposefully
choose to quiet our hearts. As we spend time reading the
Bible and praying, we become attuned to His voice. The more
we listen and obey, the more He speaks. Any relationship
grows over time through communication. Listen. The Lord is
speaking. Can you hear Him?

Dear Lord, may I be like Samuel and desire to hear You speak.
Help me set aside quiet time each day to spend with You.
Give me ears to hear and a heart to follow. Amen.

Speak to Me

In the beginning was the Word, and the
Word was with God, and the Word was God.
JOHN 1:1 KJV

A baby's first words are monumental for any parent. Slowly, the baby's brain is developed enough to not only recognize and interpret words and phrases, but to create understanding and use words in the correct context.

Some parents jokingly admit that they would be content going back to a time when their chatterbox toddler or especially stubborn middle school student had no speaking ability whatsoever. With the ability to speak comes the opportunity to say such impacting yet diverse phrases as "I love you" or "I hate you." Words are powerful!

When the apostle John wrote about Jesus, he referred to Him as "the Word." Another way to understand "the Word" is to recognize that Jesus is the Truth. If something is true, it means that it is unchanging. John wanted readers to understand that Jesus stays the same, no matter what.

As our children grow and change, we can be reminded that their growing knowledge should always be based on "the Word"—God's Truth.

Lord, help me teach my children about
Your constant love and truth. Amen.

Your Special Dwelling Place

"In My Father's house are many dwelling places; if it were not so, I would have told you; for I go to prepare a place for you."

JOHN 14:2 NASB

Moms spend much of their time maintaining their home: cooking, cleaning, laundering. . .the list is endless. Because sin entered into the world, work came along as a consequence. Even now you may be wondering what to make for dinner and if you should grab that pack of chicken from the freezer so it can thaw.

But take a moment to rest in the promise Jesus gave in John 14:2. He informs us that there is a place waiting for us that will require nothing on our part. Jesus tells us that in His Father's house, there are plenty of rooms for everyone—there will be a place tailor-made for you.

What a joy to know that He has found time to prepare a place for *you*. . .one that you will never have to worry about cleaning!

Jesus, please give me strength to maintain my earthly home, but also help me remember the special home that You have prepared for me in heaven. Amen.

Running for Comfort

Have mercy on me, my God, have mercy on me,
for in you I take refuge. I will take refuge in the
shadow of your wings until the disaster has passed.

PSALM 57:1 NIV

The mother woke to the sound of tiny feet pattering across the floor. Lifting the covers, she pulled her trembling child into bed with her. She cuddled him close, his small hands fisted in her nightgown.

Each night when her child woke from a nightmare, the mother held him, comforting him with soothing words. In this safe embrace, he found peace once again.

Often, events in our lives can be upsetting, sometimes terrifying. We tremble in fear, our peace and contentment far away. The struggle can become unbearable if we try to be brave and solve the problem on our own.

Our only hope is to run through the dark to God, lifting our hands to Him. With words of comfort, God lets us know He will care for us. We don't need to fear anything. He will always soothe us and give us peace.

Thank You, Lord, that I can run to You
for comfort when life gets scary. Amen.

God-Focused Priorities

Delight thyself also in the LORD: and he shall give thee the desires of thine heart. Commit thy way unto the LORD; trust also in him; and he shall bring it to pass.

PSALM 37:4–5 KJV

With what or whom do you delight or take pleasure? Good movies, shopping, conversation with girlfriends? How do these activities shape your priorities?

The Lord tells us to delight or take pleasure in Him. But how do we delight in Him? We spend time getting to know the Lord more intimately through daily quiet time, reading and studying the Bible, continual prayer, and corporate worship. However, how often have you thought, *I am way too busy to be engaged in these spiritual disciplines—I have a child!*

It is precisely because we are so busy that it is imperative to spend time with the Lord. Spiritual disciplines enable us to align our priorities with His will. As we know the Lord more intimately, our desires become one with His.

Gracious Lord, I surrender my priorities to You and ask that You would align them with Your priorities, Your best for my family and me. Amen.

Keep It Simple, Be Consistent

"But let your statement be, 'Yes, yes' or
'No, no'; anything beyond these is of evil."
MATTHEW 5:37 NASB

Our Lord's clear say-what-you-mean-and-mean-what-you-say approach is the best to use when teaching and training small children. Instant obedience is more easily achieved when requests are clear, short, and specific.

For example, instead of saying, "Pick up your toys and put them away," we can say, "Put your truck in the toy box." This clear direction eliminates choice and makes it easier for the child to obey. Either the truck is in the toy box or it isn't.

Simple directives also make it easier for mothers to remain consistent. With too many words, misunderstandings may arise, you forgetting exactly what you said or the child not fully understanding the direction.

Making our "yes" a true yes and our "no" a true no will make our lives simpler.

Anything more may mean trouble for little ones and busy mothers.

O Father, remind me to talk less, to say what I mean,
and to mean what I say. Help me to be consistent
with my training and directions so my children
learn obedience and godliness. Amen.

The Perfume of Sacrifice

Live a life filled with love, following the example of Christ. He loved us and offered himself as a sacrifice for us, a pleasing aroma to God.

EPHESIANS 5:2 NLT

Today, perfume is an exciting, feminine luxury. It can be either a pleasant scent worn daily or a glamorous accessory to eveningwear.

In biblical times, perfume was given as a gift at the birth of Christ and later was sacrificially used to anoint Him before His death. We are told in Ephesians 5 that true love is following the example of Christ and loving others sacrificially. That sacrifice of love is like a perfume, a pleasing aroma to God.

Once a woman becomes a mom, she lives her life, even the mundane duties of each day, for someone else, and sometimes feels personally lost in the shuffle. The truth is, God takes great pleasure in the sweet scent that wafts before His throne, which can only come from the type of love that incites great sacrifice.

Your sacrificial love is like perfume, pleasing the senses of God.

Lord, help me remember that my daily sacrifices are precious to You, as precious as the sweetest perfume. Amen.

Childlike Praise

*He has given me a new song to sing, a hymn of praise
to our God. Many will see what he has done and be
amazed. They will put their trust in the Lord.*

PSALM 40:3 NLT

When a baby says his or her first word, most mothers react
as though the evening news should be contacted. The little
one is now not only vocal through cries but also through
words. These words will eventually be strung together to form
sentences, even songs.

Children singing reflect a lightheartedness that adults
lose all too quickly. One day, children will reach an age when
their singing no longer reflects carefree innocence. They are
either told they have mediocre musical talent, that they could
make big money on the next nationwide televised event, or
that their singing should be reserved only for church.

But the Bible says that God created us to praise Him. He
gives us new songs for different circumstances and seasons.
Whether musically inclined or not, we can bless God's heart
by singing loudly—with our children.

*Lord, thank You for filling my heart with praise, help me sing
with the carefree voice of a child—Your child. Amen.*

Sincerity

Love must be sincere.
ROMANS 12:9 NIV

Attempting to disguise her anger, a young mother addressed her child in a singsong tone of voice. Her child responded by saying, "Mom, I know you're mad, you don't have to pretend you're not." Even the tone of our voice cannot mask our emotions.

Love must also come from the heart. It must be sincere—genuine. People can tell the difference. We may be wearing a smile. We may be saying the proper words. We may be doing the right things. Yet, if our heart does not match our outward demeanor, others quickly detect the inconsistency.

There is a solution. First, we can receive God's love. Then we can allow the Lord to change our heart by making it more like His. He is the Potter; we are the clay. When we choose to be pliable, He molds and shapes our heart. This is not an overnight process. Yet gradually our words and actions will flow from the heart, then everything else falls into place.

Dear Lord, change my heart and make it like Yours.
Then my love will be sincere and my words
will bring glory to You. Amen.

Distractions from Our True Calling

"Everyone who is called by My name,
And whom I have created for My glory. . ."
ISAIAH 43:7 NASB

Isaiah reminds us that our true calling or purpose in life is to glorify God. God created us for His glory, honor, reputation, or splendor. Therefore, we must seek the Lord's face to determine our calling for this season of our lives. God will reveal His purpose for us, instructing and teaching us in the way we should go, counseling us with His eye upon us (Psalm 32:8).

The challenge lies in choosing to say yes to the activities that align with His purpose and no to those that do not. We must remember that when we say yes to a *good* activity, we are implicitly saying no to a *best* activity. . .time with our family or time doing what is truly our calling. This doesn't come easy, but it may help to remember that motherhood of a preschooler is for a short season, gone forever before we know it.

Lord, I invite You to reveal Your purpose for me. Align my days, raising my child with activities that glorify You. Amen.

Fear Not

For God hath not given us the spirit of fear;
but of power, and of love, and of a sound mind.
2 TIMOTHY 1:7 KJV

As our children develop, they learn many important lessons from their mothers. They come to know danger and how to respect the many perils in life. However, we can also impart unnecessary trepidations to our children, ones that will hinder them as they grow.

Sometimes we fear the unknown, the power of rejection, or even failure. If we aren't careful, we can forfeit great blessings by ignoring God's urging to serve in the work He has designed for us.

What an exciting gift we could give God if we were to stand on the proverbial edge of the cliff, ready to step out in power and love to serve God. Let us have a mind set on God, not on our own inadequacies. Let's be content wherever His path leads.

Thank You, Lord, that You can take all fear from me.
Give me the desire to serve You in any area You want. Amen.

A Rocky Start

Then Jesus got into the boat and started across the lake with his disciples. Suddenly, a fierce storm struck the lake, with waves breaking into the boat. But Jesus was sleeping.

MATTHEW 8:23-24 NLT

Jo and her husband, David, were beyond excited. It was the first family vacation to the lake in a long time. After reaching their cabin, hauling a few bags inside, and changing, everyone made their way down to the water. Their oldest dove right in, but their youngest, Josh, held back. At three years old, the most water he'd ever seen was in the bathtub. Now, as he stared at the water rushing in over his toes, he began to cry.

"Help, Mommy! Daddy!"

Jo and David kept eyes on the oldest while paying special attention to their youngest. David waded toward Josh, lifted him up in his arms, and bounced so the water made them both wet.

Jo waded nearby and called to Josh. "See, Josh, you're safe with Daddy!"

Jesus' disciples felt the same way as Josh: alone and terrified. But Jesus was right there and would never have abandoned them in their fear.

God, thank You for protecting me. Amen.

Out of Our Comfort Zones

Indeed, we felt we had received the sentence of death.
But this happened that we might not rely on
ourselves but on God, who raises the dead.

2 CORINTHIANS 1:9 NIV

We all enjoy familiar surroundings and predictable outcomes. Friends are chosen over strangers. Home is preferred over hotels. When our environment is somewhat controlled, *we* feel more in control. But when we step out of our comfort zone, anything can happen! It's scary. It's intimidating. It's humbling.

Many times God calls us out of our comfort zones for that very reason. He wants us to venture out of the boat, like Peter. He knows that we will have to trust Him alone and not rely upon ourselves. He wants us to become God-sufficient, not self-sufficient.

The next time God takes you to an uncomfortable place, view it as an opportunity for spiritual growth. Rely totally upon Him. Then, watch God work in amazing ways!

Dear Lord, help me follow You when I am
called out of my comfort zone. Teach me
to rely upon You and not myself. Amen.

Tug-of-War

*No, dear brothers and sisters, I have not achieved it,
but I focus on this one thing: Forgetting the past
and looking forward to what lies ahead.*

PHILIPPIANS 3:13 NLT

In tug-of-war, there are two sides, each pulling on one end of a rope, hoping to pull the other side across a line. Our enemy wants us to remain in a never-ending battle with our past, because it keeps us from moving on to the future. Our enemy is relentless; he will pull until he entraps you in the game.

Let go of the rope and watch your past flail as it falls away. It may taunt you and try to lure you back, but ignore it.

As parents, we need to learn from the past, but then we need to take our growth into the future. Letting go of regrets and failures, while we take what was meant for evil and use it for good, will help us make wise parenting decisions and train up our children in the way they should go.

---

*Father, forgive me for the things I have done that
disappointed You. Help me to receive Your forgiveness
and move on, fully, into the future. Amen.*

Strength in Grace

*You therefore, my son, be strong
in the grace that is in Christ Jesus.*

2 TIMOTHY 2:1 NKJV

The mother watched her child take his first hesitant steps. After tumbling to the ground, his eyes turned to her, seeking a reaction. Her obvious joy at his success, not his fall, encouraged the child to try again. Each time he tried, he grew stronger. Before long, the child's steps were no longer hesitant, but confident.

By not displaying concern, but showing encouragement, the mother gave her son the strength to climb back up and try again. The boy trusted her for his well-being. He continued to learn to walk, and then to run.

As Christians, we often fall or make mistakes. God's grace is always there to demonstrate His forgiveness. He urges us to climb to our feet and try again. With God in charge of our well-being, we can not only have the ability to walk, we can learn to run with confidence in God.

---

*Dear Father, thank You for Your grace, which encourages me
to grow stronger in my faith and in my walk. Continue to
help me find strength and confidence in You. Amen.*

Smile!

*Why art thou cast down, O my soul? and why art thou
disquieted in me? hope thou in God: for I shall yet
praise him for the help of his countenance.*

PSALM 42:5 KJV

Although we cannot see God's face with our physical eyes,
our spiritual eyes can perceive His countenance. As we spend
time in His presence, our agitation is calmed; our anxiety,
eased.

As we are helped by the countenance of the Father, so
children are helped by the countenance of the mother. As the
Father's ambassador to her children, a mother can encourage
a child with just a loving look. Or she can discourage her
children with a knit brow, a slight frown, or a quiet sigh.

The best defense against a sad countenance is a smile.
Watch what happens when you smile at your little ones. They
will naturally smile back. When Mom is smiling, the whole
house will be full of light.

---

*Father, thank You for shining Your face on me.
Let me lift up my little ones daily with a bright
countenance. Help me to smile through the storms
of life, knowing that You are always with me. Amen.*

Peaceful Parenting

You will keep in perfect peace those whose minds
are steadfast, because they trust in you.
ISAIAH 26:3 NIV

God's Word directs us to set our minds and hearts on things that are above (Colossians 3:1-2). We need to be deliberate in concentrating or focusing our minds on God's eternal perspective, not on the temporal earthly perspective.

God tells us that when our minds are steadfast or fixed on Him, we will have peace. When our hearts and minds turn to the Lord for wisdom, guidance, and instruction in parenting, He will sustain us. We will receive peace not because we understand fully what is occurring in our world or will happen in the future, but because we trust the Lord.

In parenting, as we have this eternal perspective, we can know the Lord's perfect peace. We can be free from our fears, inadequacies, insecurities, and worries about our children, parenting, and the future, knowing the Lord has a plan for our welfare that provides a future with hope for our family and us (Jeremiah 29:11).

Lord, I praise You for the peace provided in parenting
as I trust in Your eternal perspective. Amen.

Take It to the Lord

"Come to me, all you who are weary
and burdened, and I will give you rest."
MATTHEW 11:28 NIV

Victoria looked at her calendar. *Parent-Teacher Meeting 6:00 p.m.* glared up at her in red ink. She sighed, wishing she didn't have to attend. As she dressed for work, her mind raced with all she needed to do that day. After work, dinner had to be prepared and cleaned up. After the conference, she would rush home and bake cupcakes for her daughter's class, do laundry, and work on her Sunday school lesson. On top of her regular job, getting the kids to school, and keeping the house, her time was evaporating before her eyes. Why hadn't she said no to some of the demanding things that awaited her?

Victoria bowed her head and prayed.

Father, sometimes I feel overburdened with all the things I need to get done. I thank You that I can come to You, and You will make me feel so much better. Please teach me to say no sometimes so that I will stay refreshed. In Jesus' name, amen.

*Fix these words of mine in your hearts and minds;
tie them as symbols on your hands and bind them
on your foreheads. Teach them to your children.*

DEUTERONOMY 11:18–19 NIV

If you attended Sunday school as a child, you most likely recall hearing the stories of Daniel in the lions' den, David and Goliath, and Noah and the ark. You probably also sang songs such as "This Little Light of Mine" and, of course, "Jesus Loves Me."

God told the Israelites to remember His teachings and to teach them to their children. Moms (and dads too!) are to be instructing kids in the ways of the Lord. However, regularly attending a place of worship is a wonderful supplement to effectively training them. If you already have a class where your children can learn more about Jesus, remember to thank their teacher this Sunday. If you don't currently attend a place of worship, consider finding one where your children can grow in their knowledge of Jesus.

---

*Lord Jesus, thank You that Your words have been passed
down through the generations. I pray for knowledge and
for clarity as I teach them to my children. Amen.*

And Jesus grew in wisdom and stature,
and in favor with God and man.
LUKE 2:52 NIV

When Lisa prepared to be a mother for the first time, she was a bit nervous, but she was also confident that she knew what she was doing. She'd purchased all the latest parenting books, had the safest childproof amenities, and had even been trained in infant CPR. What more would she need?

The evening the baby arrived, however, Lisa realized she didn't have a clue what she was doing. What if she wasn't a good parent? What if her child grew to be one of those wanted people on the evening news? Such thoughts and fears seemed silly to her before, but now they bombarded her already fatigued mind.

Lying in bed, Lisa remembered she wasn't alone. God would ultimately determine her baby's future, but she could be a loving and positive model for him. One day he would hopefully become a man whose heart's desire was for wisdom and God.

God, guide me as I guide my child. Amen.

Be a Faithful Steward

Moreover it is required in stewards,
that a man be found faithful.

1 CORINTHIANS 4:2 KJV

Although many might think of children as our possessions, we are only stewards of their little lives. God has graciously loaned us precious souls to prepare for eternity.

We are to love them (Titus 2:4), to provide their physical needs (Proverbs 31:21), to teach them God's Word all day (Deuteronomy 6:7), and to instruct them in God's law (Proverbs 1:8).

Being a steward is not easy, as Joseph discovered. Yet no matter what his situation, he remained steadfast in his faith, knowing God was always with him—protecting him, guiding him, providing for him. And because of his faith, things always worked out in his favor and, in turn, in favor of his family.

We also must have courage, remain true to our task, and exercise faith, believing that God will indeed help us as we take on this awesome responsibility because we love Him.

Dear Lord, because I know that You are forever
beside me, I rise up in faith, knowing You work out all
things in my favor and the favor of my family. Amen.

Family Celebration

One generation shall praise thy works to another,
and shall declare thy mighty acts.

PSALM 145:4 KJV

"Jesus loves me, this I know!"

Several children yelled the song at the top of their lungs as they stood before the congregation. One mom sitting near the front breathed a sigh of relief that her boys did not stand side by side. Another mother prayed her daughter would not pick her nose. But all the parents felt like cheering God for these beautiful, bright-eyed little singers.

Other generations of Christians in the congregation celebrated Jesus' love as they listened to the children's praise. A teenager remembered meeting God in Bible school. A middle-aged woman hurting from divorce took refuge in the knowledge that God still loved her. An elderly man realized afresh the God of his childhood still kept the promises in His Word.

"The Bible tells me so!" The kids gave it their all. The children wandered off the platform to enthusiastic applause.

Up in heaven, God clapped His hands too.

Lord God, how great You are! How wonderful to celebrate
Your love as a church family. Someday all generations
will worship You together forever! Amen.

Freed Captives

O give thanks unto the Lord, for he is good. . .
Let the redeemed of the Lord say so, whom he
hath redeemed from the hand of the enemy.

PSALM 107:1-2 KJV

Young children often do something wrong that requires punishment. As mothers, we are usually the ones who deal with each infraction. The toddler never wants to face up to what he or she has done. They cry huge tears to garner sympathy as they act like they are being imprisoned. Most of the time when the chastisement is completed, children seek affirmation that they are still loved, despite what they have done.

Before we were Christians, we were held captive by sin. We couldn't set ourselves free; we could only receive a pardon by accepting Christ as our Savior. When we did, the change in our lives was dramatic. We knew we were loved by the God who created everything. The freedom we have in Christ is so overwhelming that we can't help but be thankful.

Lord, I can't say enough about how You paid the price
for my sin. Thank You, Jesus, for redeeming me. Amen.

Wisdom

When pride comes, then comes disgrace,
but with humility comes wisdom.
PROVERBS 11:2 NIV

Wisdom is a coveted virtue. When the Lord asked King Solomon what he most desired, King Solomon chose wisdom. God granted him a wise and discerning heart. Although worldly wisdom may come with age, spiritual wisdom does not. Many young women are more spiritually discerning than their mothers or even grandmothers. How is that possible?

Spiritual wisdom comes with spiritual maturity. Spiritual maturity comes from an intimate walk with the Lord. Since God is the source of wisdom, we must humbly ask that He impart His wisdom to us. We must acknowledge that He knows best.

Mothers of young children can easily become overwhelmed. Discipline issues and sibling rivalry require wisdom that we may not possess. Chapter one of James encourages those that lack wisdom to ask God. We must not doubt, but believe that God will impart His wisdom to us. Do not try to tackle motherhood alone. Humble yourself before the Lord and His wisdom will be yours.

Dear Lord, You know there are some days I feel
inadequate. Help me humbly come before You
so that I can receive Your wisdom. Amen.

Help Me Raise Them Right!

But the fruit of the Spirit is love, joy, peace,
patience, kindness, goodness, faithfulness.
GALATIANS 5:22 NASB

Tiffany hoped that the church counselor would be able to help her teach the boys how to love and treat each other better. With tears in her eyes, she explained, "My boys fight over the blocks, the cars, the puzzles, and they even fight over their books. I don't know what to do about the twins. Everyone told me when I was pregnant that the babies would be so close and loving. Boy, were they wrong."

"So your boys never get along?" The counselor asked.

Tiffany sniffed. "Well, I wouldn't say *never*."

Later, she left feeling better. One of the things she took away from the meeting was that the boys were expressing themselves, and that with a little loving care from her and a lot of help from God, they would grow into the young Christian men she envisioned.

Heavenly Father, be with me, and help me to raise my
children so that they will be women and men of God. Amen.

A Good Example

Care for the flock that God has entrusted to you. Watch
over it willingly, not grudgingly. . .because you are eager
to serve God. . . lead them by your own good example.

1 PETER 5:2–3 NLT

As a mom, God has given you the opportunity to be an example to your little one. Sure, we all fall short. . .especially when yet *another* cup of milk spills, or when the wall is "decorated" with crayon. But overall, you are vital in the development of that little human being—his health, his education, his emotions, and most of all, his spiritual training. What you do will be absorbed—and most often imitated—by him. Your choice to be a good example will have long-lasting benefits.

In 1 Peter, there is a charge to church leaders to care for those under them. However, as moms, this applies to us as well. We have our own little "flock" to care for—those wonderful children God has entrusted to us.

Lord, I pray that I will reflect You today as
I strive to be a good example to the ones
whom You have entrusted to me. Amen.

Renewed Mind

Whatever you do, work at it with all your heart,
as working for the Lord, not for human masters.
COLOSSIANS 3:23 NIV

Claire recalled the infinite number of diapers changed, loads of laundry completed, dishes washed, house cleanings, meals prepared, times of instruction with her children—and thought to herself, *Isn't there more to life than this?*

The Lord tells us, "YES!" The Lord provides a renewed mind-set for how we are to embrace these tasks as mothers. He instructs us that whatever our task (e.g., cleaning toilets, grocery shopping, teaching our children), we need to put our entire being into it as if we were polishing the pearly gates for the Almighty! We are, in fact, serving Him when we engage in the very tasks the Lord has specifically called us to do for this season of our life. We can choose to complete His work with an attitude of drudgery and boredom, or we can reframe the task as giving back to the One who has blessed us with a home and children who call us "Mother."

Lord, renew my mind to complete every task for Your glory
in thankfulness for the blessing of being a mom. Amen.

Immersed in God's Word

I will delight myself in thy statutes:
I will not forget thy word.
PSALM 119:16 KJV

In today's fast-paced world, it is difficult to find delight in much of anything. We just don't have time. So how can we really delight in God's Word? Often we read it because it's the "right thing" to do. We want to set the right example for our little ones, or we want God's blessing on our family. We figure that's the best way to get it.

It's true that God does bless those who recognize the importance of His Word and of spending time with Him, but we shouldn't be using our devotions as a magic formula to get something from Him. Our desire should be to become more like Christ. The only way to do this is to walk with Him daily. We must learn more about Him and put into practice what we observe. Then we not only reap God's blessing, we become one of His blessings. That's the best legacy we can give to our children.

Thank You, Lord, for giving me Your Word that I might know You more fully and become more like You. Amen.

Rules

But speak thou the things which become sound doctrine.
TITUS 2:1 KJV

Four-year-old Allen slammed the door to the car then buckled up his seat belt. He looked at his mom and announced, "I don't want to go to school anymore." He crossed his arms and stared straight ahead.

"Why not? Did you have a bad day?" Laura watched her son's eyes fill with tears.

"They have too many rules at school," he blurted out.

"I agree," Laura answered. She prayed for the right words to help her explain the importance of rules.

Allen perked up. "You do?"

"Sure. You can't go down the slide backward because you might hit your head on the ground. I know they won't let you run with pencils—you might stab yourself or someone else. Those are horrible rules," she finished.

He uncrossed his arms. "Well, those aren't bad rules. I don't want to get hurt."

"What rules don't you like?" Laura asked as she pulled into their driveway.

Allen unfastened his seat belt. "Never mind. What are we having for a snack?"

---

*Thank You, Lord, for giving me the right words
to use when teaching my children. Amen.*

Giving Preference

Be kindly affectionate to one another with brotherly love,
in honor giving preference to one another.

ROMANS 12:10 NKJV

Children have a mind of their own. They want to do everything their way. This is very evident when they're playing with other children. We can listen to them make up new rules to adapt the game to their advantage.

Sometimes mothers get frustrated because their children will throw a fit when they don't get their way. They have to be taught that they can't change the guidelines to suit their needs alone.

As Christians, we often think our way is the right way: God's way. We justify our method and can sometimes act like two-year-olds when others don't agree. We should always consider what God's way is, but remember that there may be different roads to the same goal.

Instead of insisting on our preferences, we should pray that we can see through others' eyes. Let's be willing to honor others in matters where there might be more than one way to accomplish a goal.

Lord, help me see when to stand firm and when to be pliable.
Help me love and honor others above myself. Amen.

Open the Door

*Here I am! I stand at the door and knock. If anyone
hears my voice and opens the door, I will come in
and eat with that person, and they with me.*
REVELATION 3:20 NIV

Jesus is knocking on the door of our hearts. If we yearn for His
help, we beckon Him to enter. But if we think we can handle
life on our own, we ignore the knocking.

Whether we care to admit it or not, we desperately need
God's daily presence. His guidance, wisdom, and counsel are
invaluable. When we open our heart's door and invite Him
in, He walks with us throughout the day. Guidance is given.
Peace is imparted. Strength is obtained.

You may feel that you are handling life just fine without
His help. Are you really? God loves you so much that He gave
His life so that you can enter into a personal relationship
with Him. He's standing at the door and knocking. Why not
invite Him in?

---

*Dear Lord, thank You for pursuing a relationship with me.
May I gladly open the door to You. Amen.*

Quiet Resting Place

*"Come with me by yourselves to
a quiet place and get some rest."*

MARK 6:31 NIV

Jesus came to give us life and to have it in abundance (John 10:10). A key to living this abundant life is regular rest. God, after creating the earth and heavens, rested (Genesis 2:1–3). Jesus encouraged His disciples to have a quiet resting place. As mothers we must have a quiet resting place where we regularly spend time. This place may be in our closet, bathroom, or a special corner with a cozy chair. This place is a refuge where our children know that when Mom is in her quiet resting place, she is not to be disturbed. In our quiet resting place, we are able to fall before the glorious throne of God, pray, meditate on scripture, reflect on God's goodness, and be filled by the Lord. A basket of tools such as a Bible, devotional, tissues, journal, and pen will help facilitate our experience with the Lord in this quiet resting place.

*Father, I thank You that You have modeled an
abundant life filled with rest. Help me make
time to retreat to my quiet resting place. Amen.*

God Gives Patience and Joy

Strengthened with all might, according to his glorious power,
unto all patience and longsuffering with joyfulness.

COLOSSIANS 1:11 KJV

Apparently, newborns come with the belief that they alone
rule the world and that you exist for the sole purpose of
answering their demands. It's true that when they are tiny you
really do have to meet those needs. As they grow, however,
they begin to develop personalities. They learn the fine art
of manipulation, and the job really begins. Battles of the wills
become part of the daily routine.

Now you really have the opportunity to help your child
become what God wants her to be. It might be exasperating
at times. You have to decide if you will joyfully embrace this
chance of a lifetime or if you will wallow in the difficulties.
God knows it won't be easy. That's why He offers to give you
the strength and patience for each task. Accept His offer, and
look forward to each day with joy.

Thank You, God, for granting me the strength
and patience to joyfully raise my children.
I want o accept these gifts daily. Amen.

Builder or Vandal?

Every wise woman buildeth her house:
but the foolish plucketh it down with her hands.
PROVERBS 14:1 KJV

Building a house takes months of planning, gathering resources, and hard physical labor. Finally, however, a beautiful new house stands, complete with bedrooms where owners will rest, a kitchen from which delicious smells will draw hungry stomachs, and a living room where loved ones will open gifts around the Christmas tree. No owner would think of knocking holes in the walls or smashing the windows.

A family is hard to build too! Yet we sometimes find it easy to undermine the foundation of family faith by neglecting God's Word or His command to meet with other Christian believers. We may tear down our husbands and children with thoughtless words and actions—or let our moods blast them through the roof! When we have invested so much in building our families, why join Satan's efforts to vandalize the precious structure God has designed for His glory?

Lord Jesus, sometimes I forget how important my
family is in Your plan. Thank You for these people.
Help me be a fellow builder with You. Amen.

Lost Identity

"Since you are precious in My sight,
Since you are honored and I love you."

ISAIAH 43:4 NASB

God's Word provides our identity. Our identities are not comprised of being a mother, wife, attorney, or doctor. Rather, these are roles we may fill for a season of our lives. Our identity is in the labels Christ provided us in shedding His blood on the cross: created and formed by God, redeemed, called by name, belonging to the Lord, saved, precious, honored and loved (Isaiah 43:1–4).

The world provides a false identity to our children, encouraging them to accept the culture that says we are what we do. However, we must counter this deception of focusing on our role by grounding our children in their true identity. In living joyfully for who we are in Christ, we can teach our children a godly identity that cannot be lost. Our children can know they are called by Christ's very own name in being a Christian.

Lord, I praise You for my identity as one You created and
formed, redeemed, called by name, saved, honored, and loved.
Enable me to teach my children their identity in You. Amen.

Human Weakness Reveals God's Glory

*For we who are alive are always being given over
to death for Jesus' sake, so that his life may
also be revealed in our mortal body.*

2 CORINTHIANS 4:11 NIV

It is easy to praise the Lord when life is going well. Our newborn baby is healthy. The job offer comes through. But what is our attitude when life does not go according to our plan? The doctor discloses congenital birth defects. The door closes on our dream job. Disappointments and trials have a way of humbling us. In those moments of human weakness, we have a choice to make. We can feel sorry for ourselves and blame God or we can turn to Him, asking for His strength to persevere.

When we are at our weakest, God can reveal His strength. His power and strength uphold us. His peace sustains us. He carries us when we cannot go on. Human weakness is an opportunity to personally experience Christ's strength. May our weakness be turned to strength for His glory.

---

*Dear Lord, when I feel weak, help me lean
upon You. May others see Your strength in
me during times of weakness. Amen.*

True Hope

"Mommy? Are you awake yet?" Julie's four-year-old, Elizabeth, climbed onto her bed and poked at Julie's eyelids. Julie mumbled something that didn't even come close to the English language. Opening her eyes, Julie saw her daughter, Elizabeth, sitting cross-legged on the bed, her brown curls messy.

Julie prayed silently. It hadn't been that many hours since she'd gone to bed. What would it be like to return to childhood and be as carefree as her daughter? Still, Elizabeth's presence reminded Julie that she could have hope for the new day because of God's promises. God had blessed her not only with hope and a beautiful daughter, but with a Savior who loved her unconditionally, even if Julie wasn't always excited at the beginning of each day.

Sitting up and hugging Elizabeth, Julie thanked God for Jesus. She thanked Him for the sacrifice He had made. Julie knew that heaven would be her home one day, but for now, she thanked God for the day's treasures she hadn't even lived yet.

Jesus, my hope is in Your sacrifice. Amen.

Thankful Purpose

*Continue in prayer, and watch
in the same with thanksgiving.*
COLOSSIANS 4:2 KJV

Worry is like an invasive weed that creeps into our minds as we think about the myriad ways something can go wrong with our children. Sickness. Injury. The list goes on. Before we know it, the invasive worry becomes pervasive and consumes our thoughts. We lose our delight in our children because we are so concerned for their welfare.

Worry should not consume us and drive us from God. Instead, it should draw us to Him through prayer for each concern. Instead of dwelling on what could happen, we need to turn to Him and give thanks for His sovereignty and loving care.

We will always have concerns that involve our little ones. Our response is what makes the difference. As we come before God each time, He will give us peace for our children. Our apprehension brought before God can turn to praise. We can once more enjoy the gift of our children.

---

*Thank You, God, for turning my doubts and fears into
praise and replacing my worry with Your peace. Amen.*

The Hardest Part

Chasten thy son while there is hope,
and let not thy soul spare for his crying.
PROVERBS 19:18 KJV

Jana's little lip trembled. "But Mommy, I wanted ice cream too." Renee wavered, after all Jana was only three. Maybe she was too young to be expected to clean up her books. She pulled her child into her lap. "I wanted you to have ice cream too, but you knew the deal. Daniel picked up his things. It wouldn't be right if you were rewarded along with him," Renee explained. "I want you to remember this the next time I tell you to do something." Jana began to sob as she realized she would indeed miss out on her favorite treat.

Discipline is a hard part of parenting, but it is necessary, and if properly handled, it is quite effective. It's often difficult to be consistent or to know the best solution, but God is wise and shares this wisdom with us even in the area of child-rearing.

Dear Father, I do not like disciplining my children.
I know that I must while they are young. I only
ask for wisdom to do this properly. Amen.

Praying for Safety

*We prayed that he would give us a safe journey and
protect us, our children, and our goods as we traveled.*

EZRA 8:21 NLT

Sometimes in the hurry of travel, we don't think to ask God
to protect us on the journey. In the midst of buckling the
kids into car seats, handing out sippy cups and Cheerios,
having everyone keep their hands and feet to themselves, and
generally keeping tears at bay, we just assume that we will
make it to and from the destination without any incidents.

But have you ever taken just a moment before driving off
to ask that God protect you and your vehicle from danger?
Better yet, each time you set out on a trip, take turns with
your children, asking God to give you safety in your travels.
It's always a joy to hear the prayers of children, and what
better way to instill in them full dependence on God than to
have them request His protection? Take just a moment today
to ask your Father to protect you as you travel.

---

*Lord, thank You for Your safety as we travel.
Please protect us once again today. Amen.*

Perfect or Perfectionist?

Mark the perfect man, and behold the upright:
for the end of that man is peace.
PSALM 37:37 KJV

Motherhood is a high calling. Sometimes the height of that calling makes mothers anxious. We want to do it right. We want to be perfect, and we want our children to be perfect.

Although it is a noble goal, as we strive toward perfection, we may become perfectionists. We become intolerant of the mistakes and messes of our little ones, becoming harsh and critical, creating anxiety in the home.

Fortunately, we don't need to be perfectionists because we're already perfect. A *perfect* mother is one who is "blameless," "complete," or "has integrity." Such a mother is one who has been saved, who is blameless before God because she is in Christ.

Because she has received and understands grace, a perfect mother will understand her shortcomings and those of her children, and she will be able to impart grace to her household, giving it joy and peace.

Father, thank You for making me complete and perfect in Christ. Thank You for the grace and patience You have given me. Enable me to share this grace with my children. Amen.

So Much More

I am come that they might have life,
and that they might have it more abundantly.
JOHN 10:10 KJV

Jesus came and died on the cross to give us the gift of eternal life. But He wants to give us abundant life on earth as well. He has given us the Holy Spirit as His indwelling presence to guide, comfort, and lead. He has given us everything we need for victorious living. We can have power to rise above any situation. We can have peace in the deepest of valleys. We can experience His presence at all times.

Realize that you have not only been given eternal life, you have been given abundant life. Enjoy the blessings that Christ has in store for you, and share that joy with your children. Don't be content to live in spiritual poverty. Open the treasure chest!

Dear Lord, thank You for giving me eternal life. Help me
appropriate all the blessings that are mine so that I can
experience the abundant life that You desire for me. Amen.

Peaceful Fruit of Righteousness

No discipline seems pleasant at the time, but painful.
Later on, however, it produces a harvest of righteousness
and peace for those who have been trained by it.
HEBREWS 12:11 NIV

We often fight our heavenly Father's discipline. Discipline is the patient instruction that lovingly fosters order, peace, and a right relationship. Through conversing with the Lord, invite Him to reveal areas of your relationship with your child that need to be brought into submission to yield the peaceful fruit of righteousness. Children need structure, stability, and consistency. They need to know what they can expect for the day and be able to count on a mother who consistently and lovingly fosters obedience.

Our heavenly Father disciplines us to yield the peaceful fruit of righteousness—a right relationship with Him as Father; likewise, we need to gently and firmly teach our children a right relationship with us as mothers. As we persevere in what is often painful and unpleasant, the peaceful fruit of righteousness will be born.

Lord, reveal to me areas in which I need to lovingly instruct
my child to yield the peaceful fruit of righteousness. Amen.

Forgotten

"That's it. I've *had* it!"

Chelsea shut her screaming three-year-old in his room, placed her howling baby in his crib, and fled to the bathroom. Her children wailed. She didn't care. For sixty seconds, she would give herself the luxury of not caring if they yelled themselves blue. The week had pushed Chelsea past her limits. Her boss demanded overtime. Her husband griped about the cluttered house. Chelsea caught a virus from her children.

The pastor said God would never give Chelsea more than she could bear, but she'd like to see *him* change places with her! Tears dripped down her cheeks. *Even God has forgotten me....*

The phone rang. Chelsea sighed, unlocked the door, and picked it up.

"Chelsea?" Her Bible study leader's warm voice sounded anxious. "Are you all right? God's put you on my mind all day. Can I help?"

---

*Father, when I have nothing left to give, I somehow
think You have nothing left to give either.
Please pardon my lack of faith. Amen.*

Learning Curve

Do not think of yourself more highly than you ought, but...in accordance with the faith God has distributed to each of you.

ROMANS 12:3 NIV

Each child learns at a different rate. The doctor gives us a standard to go by when watching our toddler develop, but each child is unique. If we try to hurry our children or force them to do activities they aren't ready to do, we can cause more harm than good. When we are patient and let our toddlers go at their own pace, they have confidence in their abilities instead of always trying to do more to please their mother.

Christians grow at different paces too. Some new Christians seem to take off and mature almost overnight. Others take years to show any maturity and growth in Christ. We can't compare one believer to another because all are distinctive. If they are encouraged in their faith, instead of being criticized, Christians will become more certain of their abilities and beliefs. Let us love one another as we are, not as we think each other should be.

Thank You, Lord, that we are all special to You. Amen.

Listening Wisely

Hear instruction, and be wise, and refuse it not.
PROVERBS 8:33 KJV

Everyone has advice for mothers. From the time we are pregnant we hear how to feed, discipline, teach, dress, and love our child. Each person has a different experience or slant on what is best for us to do. Everyone is convinced that his or her opinions represent the truth.

There comes a point where a mother tunes out recommendations simply because she is overwhelmed with the variety and conflict in the various methods of child-rearing. If she listens to one person, then another will be offended.

When this happens, we must learn to listen wisely. Study God's Word and see what He says is important in child-rearing. The Bible has many good things to say to a mother. We need to hear what our friends and family are saying, but sift their counsel through scripture. Find the nuggets of truth that are good, and put away the rest. God will guide us, and He will be the final Counselor.

God, thank You for giving me wise counsel. Help me to be patient, and to truly hear what I need to know. Amen.

Judge Deborah

Now Deborah, a prophet, the wife of Lappidoth,
was leading Israel at that time. She held court under
the Palm of Deborah between Ramah and Bethel in
the hill country of Ephraim, and the Israelites went
up to her to have their disputes decided.

JUDGES 4:4–5 NIV

Bible scholars know only a few things about Deborah, Israel's only female judge: She was married, familiar with family life. She listened to people's problems and gave them God's wisdom. She was highly respected, considered one of Israel's best judges.

Oh, wouldn't it be wonderful to have a woman like Deborah in our lives? Imagine how helpful it would be, after a difficult day with a cranky little one, to visit Deborah, and ask her for God's wisdom to deal with our child!

There are many older women at church who can be our mentors, pointing us to God's wisdom. Pray that God will open your eyes to a Deborah-like woman. Finding such a friend is a blessing from the Lord, just as important today as it was four thousand years ago.

Lord, help me find a woman like Deborah
who can share Your wisdom with me. Amen.

Seeking Praise

*"His master replied, 'Well done, good and faithful
servant! You have been faithful with a few things;
I will put you in charge of many things. Come
and share your master's happiness!'"*

MATTHEW 25:23 NIV

Hot meals miraculously appear at dinnertime. Clean clothes
are folded neatly in dresser drawers. The clutter around the
house mysteriously vanishes. Who is responsible for such
occurrences—an elf or secret helper? As mothers, we all know
the answer to that question! However, many times these acts
of love are taken for granted by family members. Our efforts
seem to be in vain. Motherhood can often be a thankless job!

However, we should not become discouraged. Our husband
and children may not always express thanks and
appreciation, but the Lord will. We will receive a heavenly
reward for our behind-the-scenes acts of service. God's approving
voice will sound sweeter than that of any standing ovation.
May we yearn for God's approval, not man's applause. Live for
His praise alone.

---

*Dear Lord, help me serve my family out of my love for You.
May I yearn for Your approval. Amen.*

Choosing to Rejoice

Rejoice evermore.
1 THESSALONIANS 5:16 KJV

You wake up to freshly fallen snow sparkling in the morning sunlight. Everything is pure and perfect. It is easy to rejoice. Then you hear a croupy cough that pulls you from the frosted windowpane to your young child's bed. A quick touch to the forehead reveals what you already instinctively knew. His fever is high. You are sure it will be a trip to the doctor.

Suddenly the snow looks more like foe than friend. Will you still rejoice? You already had your day parceled out. How will you react to this change of plans? As a believer, Christ lives in you. None of this came as a surprise to Him. He allowed it for a purpose. One thing is certain: you have received the challenge to rejoice evermore. Be assured that God is with you through any trial you will face. After all, the trials and joys of this earth are but for a season. Heaven awaits, and what rejoicing that will bring.

O Lord, it is You alone who fills my heart with joy.
Thank You for sunshine in the midst of rain. Amen.

The Waiting Game

So humble yourselves under the mighty power of God,
and at the right time he will lift you up in honor.

1 PETER 5:6 NLT

High school reunions had been the worst. Not only was Jana five, ten, or fifteen years older, but it seemed she'd had to answer the same two questions that many times too.

Yes, she was married, but no, she and her husband had no children. The truth was they'd tried almost everything. . .and hadn't been able to get pregnant.

Until now.

Jana walked into her twenty-year high school reunion, one hand on her protruding abdomen. Jana flitted from friend to friend, eager to share and tell about God's faithfulness. She had no idea why God's timing wasn't her and her husband's timing. But maybe God was glorifying Himself through the testimony Jana was now excitedly giving her friends and family. Within days of learning they were pregnant, Jana had received more exciting news. Their adoption efforts were finally coming to an end. They would adopt a three-year-old girl just weeks after Jana gave birth to their newborn daughter.

Father, Your faithfulness astounds me.
I will praise You for Your timing. Amen.

Grown-Up Love

*When I was a child, I spake as a child, I understood
as a child, I thought as a child: but when I became
a man, I put away childish things.*

1 CORINTHIANS 13:11 KJV

Pastors often read 1 Corinthians 13, the "Love Chapter," at weddings. Even unbelievers feel drawn to the rich poetic language, vivid imagery, and most of all, to that magic word: love. Christians, upon hearing the powerful Word of God, recommit their lifestyles to Christ.

But God uses families to help us understand our lack of love! A mom can read all day about long-suffering, but when her four-year-old uses lipstick to paint the living room walls, she stops theorizing about patience. We mothers consider ourselves kind women until our toddlers hide the car keys.

Fortunately, God knows we, too, are still children. Believers won't mature completely until "that which is perfect is come" (1 Corinthians 13:10 KJV). We may find the road to true love a long one. But with the help of God's Spirit, we will see ourselves, more and more, in the Love Chapter.

---

*Lord Jesus, when I feel the least loving,
remind me how it is done. Thank You. Amen.*

Whose Yoke Are You Bearing?

For my yoke is easy, and my burden is light.
MATTHEW 11:30 KJV

Despite living in a world with so many conveniences, women seem to be under a greater burden now than ever before. Mothers seem especially stressed. They are constantly on the run for their families and themselves. They are frustrated because they can't meet the maternal standards of their mothers and grandmothers, nor can they achieve the exhilaration of "liberation" touted by the world.

If the yoke is too heavy, it may not be the one He's fashioned for us. It may be one we've made ourselves. Jesus said *His* burden is light. We can sometimes make our yokes heavier by expecting perfection, by trying to please others rather than God, and by seeking fulfillment outside of God's plan. Jesus will help us carry our burden, even if we've added more to it.

Father, I know I have added to the burden You want me to carry. Give me the strength to drop the nonessentials so I can carry Your lighter yoke. Amen.

Counted Faithful

And I thank Christ Jesus our Lord, who hath enabled me,
for that he counted me faithful, putting me into the ministry.
1 TIMOTHY 1:12 KJV

It is true that in this passage Paul is talking about being a minister of the Bible, but what he says can be applied in many ways to motherhood. We certainly should teach the Gospel to our children. Those are the most important lessons they will ever have because that training will impact their eternity.

There are obvious ways mothers care for children, such as providing meals and clean clothes, but there are subtle ways as well. We must be careful how we respond to each situation in life, because our kids are watching and learning. We are always teaching them, even when we don't realize it.

It is an awesome task, but Christ enables us. He saw something in each of us that said, "This woman will be faithful." His strength will never fail us. Through Him we can be worthy of our call to motherhood.

Dear Jesus, I am honored that You find me
worthy to be a mother to Your little ones.
Help me be faithful in this ministry. Amen.

God's Instruction Book

*But the wisdom that comes from heaven is first of all pure;
then peace-loving, considerate, submissive, full of mercy
and good fruit, impartial and sincere.*

JAMES 3:17 NIV

As each day of rearing a child passed, Laura felt more and more inadequate. *God provided the child,* Laura thought, *shouldn't He also provide the instruction book?*

God does provide the instruction book: the Bible. James 1:5 (ESV) tells us, "If any of you lacks wisdom, let him ask God, who gives generously to all without reproach, and it will be given him." When we struggle with feelings of inadequacy and failure as a mom, we can study God's instruction book, converse with God regarding the areas where we need wisdom, and then enjoy the wisdom the Lord will provide that is "first of all pure; then peace-loving, considerate, submissive, full of mercy and good fruit, impartial and sincere" (James 3:17 NIV).

---

*Lord, thank You for the child You have given me.
Please provide me with wisdom in the specific areas
in which I feel inadequate as a mom. Amen.*

Grasp His Love

And I pray that you, being rooted and established
in love, may have power, together with all the
Lord's holy people, to grasp how wide and long
and high and deep is the love of Christ.

Ephesians 3:17–18 niv

Sometimes the whole world seems to be against us. Abandoned by family or friends, we sense that we're all alone. Although intellectually we may concede that we haven't been totally forsaken, our emotions tell us otherwise.

When we find ourselves in that lonely state, we must grasp the truth about love. God is love. God's love will never fail. He demonstrated that love by laying down His life for us. How great is that love! Nothing will ever be able to separate us from God's love. He loves us in the good times as well as the bad. His love is unconditional. He cannot love us any more or any less than He always does. How awesome is God's love! May we truly grasp and experience His amazing love.

Dear Lord, thank You for Your unfailing love!
Help me fully receive Your unconditional love
so that I will never feel unloved again. Amen.

Counterfeit Fillers

So God created mankind in his own image, in the image of God he created them; male and female he created them.

GENESIS 1:27 NIV

Motherhood can sometimes foster feelings of emptiness, particularly when many of the tasks we do day after day for our child become chores. In fact, we may even try to run from the void inside by doing more—joining every playgroup, doing every service project, filling our day with more and more busyness. Or we dwell on how life will be better when our child is older and we have more time for ourselves! However, these activities and daydreams are counterfeit fillers. At best, counterfeits provide only brief, fleeting satisfaction.

The Lord is the only permanent and genuine filler for the emptiness we feel. God created us in His image with the intent that we would need Him to fill any emptiness we may have. God promises that He will fill us (Matthew 5:6; Isaiah 29:19; 55:1-3) when we seek Him. Reject counterfeits. Seek Him alone.

Lord, in this season of raising my child, help me to be aware of counterfeit fillers and seek You alone. Come fill me. Amen.

Dependable as the Sunrise

*It is of the LORD's mercies that we are not consumed,
because his compassions fail not. They are new
every morning: great is thy faithfulness.*

LAMENTATIONS 3:22–23 KJV

"Look, Mommy!" The four-year-old wriggled free from Elena's grasp in the early morning chill and pointed toward the east. "God likes to finger paint too!"

The glorious rose, lavender, and peach clouds formed a canopy fit for the golden sun, which was enthroned on the horizon like a king. *Oh, Lord, You are such an artist!* How long had it been since Elena had stopped during the morning rush to enjoy the sunrise God designed?

What if God decided to close down the dawn every time His work went unnoticed? The earth and its inhabitants would not survive long. Yet despite our failure to love and worship Him, God does not waver in His compassion for His people. Even when we do not appreciate His mercies, fresh and new every morning, He sends the warmth and beauty we take for granted.

---

*Lord Jesus, thank You for the beautiful sunrise.
You are the faithful Sun of Righteousness, who makes
salvation possible for my family and me. Amen.*

A Gentle and Quiet Spirit

*Clothe yourselves. . .with the beauty that comes
from within, the unfading beauty of a gentle
and quiet spirit, which is so precious to God.*

1 PETER 3:4 NLT

"Gentle" and "quiet" are not words we moms typically have spring to our minds. In fact, some days are spent trying to block out the noise of the two-year-old shouting the ABCs or repeatedly reminding the three-year-old to stop pulling the cat's tail.

God's Word instructs us to focus on the beauty within us—a "gentle and quiet spirit," which has a beauty that will never fade. What a joy it would be to be known by our children and by others as one who has a gentle and quiet spirit, but mostly as "precious to God."

The more we work on developing a gentle and quiet spirit, the easier those days will seem when the four-year-old "helps" by watering the plants—a little too much—or the baby has lost her pacifier *again*.

---

*Lord, please help me put on a gentle and quiet spirit
today. Today we focus so much on outward beauty,
remind me to emphasize the inner beauty,
which You consider "precious." Amen.*

No Excuses

Patient endurance is what you need now,
so that you will continue to do God's will.
Then you will receive all that he has promised.
HEBREWS 10:36 NLT

It was a small argument this time, but Barbara knew it was one her son shouldn't have heard. He sat quietly, playing with his blocks. She sighed. At the age of four, Andy had heard his parents arguing way too often. The things she and her husband fought over were silly. Why couldn't she just cool her temper and discuss things calmly with her husband, maybe give in every now and then?

Hadn't her husband joked with her last Sunday that maybe they should take the anger management class offered at the church? Barbara decided that now was as good a time as any to start agreeing with her husband. She kissed Andy's forehead and then returned him to his toys. Barbara picked up her cell phone and dialed the church office.

Heavenly Father, thank You for helping me to
learn patience as I walk down this road of life.
Without You I would be lost. Amen.

One Flesh, First and Last

Therefore shall a man leave his father and his mother,
and shall cleave unto his wife: and they shall be one flesh.

GENESIS 2:24 KJV

Something happens to a wife once she becomes a mother. Her focus often shifts to the baby, sometimes to the exclusion of her husband. As more children come along, she sees herself as a mother first and a wife second.

This is not God's plan. While children are an integral part of His design, when God gave Eve to Adam, the first family was complete. The children would come and go, but they would be one flesh, first and last.

During those hectic years when the children are small and demanding, set aside time for your husband, and teach the children to honor that time. He needs your support and encouragement even more as a father than he did when he was a husband only.

And you need him just as much.

Father, my husband is precious to me, but sometimes
I forget him as I get consumed with the needs of these
little ones You've given me. Help me to keep
him first, so our love will last. Amen.

Not Mine

*And the multitude of them that believed were of one
heart and of one soul...they had all things common.*

ACTS 4:32 KJV

One of the first words our children learn is "mine." We notice
it especially when they are playing with another child. Our
little one can turn into an ogre as she grabs onto her toy and
refuses to share.

Teaching children to share can be an arduous task. They
get angry when another child wants their toy. Our children
don't understand the concept of letting someone else have a
turn.

Sometimes Christians act like toddlers over what they
consider theirs in the body of believers. "Nobody sits in my
pew." "This is my area of ministry. How could she try to barge
in and do what I do so well?"

God wants us to share all things as a group. We need
to take turns doing jobs. When we allow others to share and
work alongside us, we have real peace and joy because we are
behaving in a godly manner. Let's rejoice in others and not be
possessive.

---

*Lord, thank You for making us a body that
fits together and works together. Amen.*

He writes the same way in all his letters, speaking in them of these matters. His letters contain some things that are hard to understand, which ignorant and unstable people distort, as they do the other Scriptures, to their own destruction.

2 PETER 3:16 NIV

"He started it!" Shawna's twin boys shouted at the same time. They both pointed their index finger at the other.

"One at a time! One at a time!" Shawna commanded, feeling as though her services as a mother would have prepared her well for a Supreme Court seat.

Both boys began talking, their explanations conflicting. Shawna didn't know what had happened, and there was no way she was going to find out until she separated the two. Maybe then she would be able to understand the truth.

Today's world, its beliefs and opinions, is a lot like fighting children. The truth is hard to distinguish apart from God's wisdom. When Paul wrote his letters, he wrote with wisdom, but those who did not believe were not able to understand.

Ask God for wisdom, understanding, and discernment as you study the scriptures and seek truth.

God, help me to understand Your truth. Amen.

I have called you friends.
JOHN 15:15 KJV

It may seem too early to choose good friends for your youngster, but this is the perfect time to begin teaching him the importance of selecting positive influences. Of course, he cannot do it by himself yet, but he can recognize good traits when they are pointed out. "I like the way Alex shares," you may say, or, "Isn't Shawn good at waiting his turn?" There are many valuable life lessons to be learned, beginning at an early age.

Even more important than growing earthly relationships is developing his relationship with his heavenly Father. Remind him, "Jesus is your very best Friend." Daily Bible reading and prayer time will strengthen his bond with this Best Friend. Share with him the importance of this Friend in your life too. By establishing this relationship, he will have a Counselor who can guide him in choosing his associates throughout life. Playmates will come and go, but Jesus will be his Friend forever.

Father, thank You for being my best Friend.
Please help me as I teach my child about You and
about those he chooses as earthly friends. Amen.

Are You Content?

But godliness with contentment is great gain.
1 TIMOTHY 6:6 KJV

It had been a hectic morning, and Kathleen just wanted a bit of time to straighten the house, so she allowed three-year-old Mallory some time with her favorite cartoons.

As she went about her tasks, she caught bits and pieces of the toy commercials that interrupted the feature program. She was growing weary of hearing "Hey kids, check this out," or "You've got to try the new." When she heard "Keep up with your friends with," she knew it was time for Mallory to be otherwise entertained.

"Mallory, why don't you come on over to the table and color for a while," Kathleen suggested.

"But Mommy, all I have are boring old crayons and paper. I need some sparkly crayons and a jumbo coloring book," Mallory whined.

Well, the season of discontent has already begun, thought Kathleen. She knew her daughter was young, but she tried to explain anyway.

"Mallory, Jesus knows what you really need, and He provides that and much more. Let's thank Him for all He's given us," she said.

O God, You do provide abundantly.
Thank You for Your many wonderful gifts. Amen.

Being Held

So do not fear, for I am with you; do not be dismayed,
for I am your God. I will strengthen you and help you;
I will uphold you with my righteous right hand.

ISAIAH 41:10 NIV

A father is running. A little boy follows close behind. As time goes on, the distance between them grows. The youngster tires and struggles to match his father's pace. Discouraged, he stops altogether. Sensing that his son has all but given up, the father stops and goes back to him. Kneeling down, he speaks to his son. Then he scoops him up and carries him home.

We may see ourselves in this scene. Closely following the Lord is difficult at times. Discouragement sets in. As we have trouble keeping up, the gap widens. We fear being lost forever. Do not be dismayed. The Lord will never leave or forsake you. He will speak encouraging words to your heart. He will pick you up and carry you like a child. He will help you by imparting His strength to you.

Dear Lord, thank You for helping me when I am weak.
May Your strength uphold me in my hour of need. Amen.

Interruptions!

Then some children were brought to Him so that He might
lay His hands on them and pray; and the disciples rebuked
them. But Jesus said, "Let the children alone, and do not
hinder them from coming to Me; for the kingdom
of heaven belongs to such as these."

MATTHEW 19:13–14 NASB

Jesus was a busy man, so the disciples felt it was their job to shoo people away. But the disciples got it all wrong. Jesus loved children! Children were the most welcome interruption of all and the real business of heaven. Jesus delighted in their childlike faith, trust, and simple joy. Children were important to Jesus.

Oh, if only we could respond to our child's interruptions as Jesus did! Instead, interruptions seem like annoyances. Our lives feel littered by so many unfinished conversations and half-done tasks. There will be time for finishing things later, Jesus suggests. For now, children are our priority.

Lord, remind me that childhood flies by. My children will
be gone soon. Let me respond to them as You would,
by stopping and opening my arms, offering time. Amen.

Lasting Fruit

"I am the vine, you are the branches; he who abides in Me and I in him, he bears much fruit, for apart from Me you can do nothing."

JOHN 15:5 NASB

God desires us to be totally connected and dependent on Him for every moment of every day, particularly as we raise the gifts the Lord has given us—our children.

The Lord describes this intimate union in John 15:1–11, as He explains how our heavenly Father is the vinegrower, deliberately growing us into the image of Christ. Jesus is the vine and we are the branches. The purpose of this union is to bear much fruit; "fruit that will last" (John 15:16 NIV) in the lives of our children to glorify God, which is what we have been created to do (Isaiah 43:7). When we as mothers model the fruit of the Spirit, our preschoolers will hunger and thirst to know the Lord, the only lasting fruit.

Lord, I praise You for the close union with You that allows me to bear lasting fruit—a personal relationship with You for my child and me. Amen.

Quiet in Chaos

And Jesus answered and said unto her, Martha, Martha,
thou art careful and troubled about many things: But one
thing is needful: and Mary hath chosen that good part,
which shall not be taken away from her.

LUKE 10:41-42 KJV

"Be a Mary, not a Martha. Don't get so busy serving the Lord that you don't have time to enjoy Him."

But where is there time in a house with toddlers? How can we sit at Jesus' feet when there isn't time to sit at all?

Perhaps our frustrations come from thinking that "sitting at Jesus' feet" is synonymous with "quiet time." There was nothing quiet about Martha and Mary's house. Jesus came with at least twelve followers. The house was crowded and noisy as Mary listened to Christ.

We can share our time in the Word—our "quiet" time—with our children. We can keep a Bible open on the table so we can read it all day long. We can pray constantly throughout the day. We don't need a silent house to hear the Lord.

Father, speak to me through the din of my day.
Tune my ears to hear You always. Amen.

Feeding One of the 5,000

*There is a lad here, which hath five
barley loaves, and two small fishes.*
JOHN 6:9 KJV

As Carrie walked her son, Colton, to the park for a picnic, his mood matched the sunshine. He couldn't wait to get on the swings and go down the slides. As they entered the park, Colton spotted an elderly man sitting on a bench with a grocery cart full of odds and ends. "Who's that man?"

Carrie led Colton out of earshot to a picnic table. She told him to stop pointing—it wasn't nice—and explained that the man probably lived in the park and he didn't have a house like theirs.

"Is he poor?" Colton asked.

"Yes." Carrie opened his lunchbox. "Here's your sandwich."

"I don't want it. I'm going to give it to the poor man. Doesn't my Bible say Jesus wants us to share?"

Colton darted toward the man, sandwich in hand.

"Colton!" Carrie yelled. He stopped, and she proudly took his hand. "I'll go with you."

---

*Father, You can accomplish great things
through small children. Help me open my
heart to Your lessons as well. Amen.*

Wise Choice

I have set before you life and death, blessing and cursing:
therefore choose life, that both thou and thy seed may live.
DEUTERONOMY 30:19 KJV

The toddler chortled as she slipped the plastic bucket over her head. It fell past her eyes. When she started forward, she ran into the wall and tumbled to the floor. As she began to cry, her mother lifted her up, explaining why she couldn't run with something over her eyes. The child repeated the behavior with the same result several times before she understood the lesson.

One of the most important decisions we face is that of choosing a life with God. Even after opting to follow Him, we often allow a blindness to send us back into an old lifestyle. When we fall, we have to remember that it was a result of our choosing.

When we shrug off the former self and walk with our eyes on God, we can walk in confidence. Our determination will not only affect us but our children and grandchildren also. Each time we choose God, we are closer to His perfection.

Lord, please forgive my past,
and lead me to a life with You. Amen.

The Best Wardrobe

Strength and honour are her clothing;
and she shall rejoice in time to come.
PROVERBS 31:25 KJV

How many times have you stood in your closet, staring at the array of sweaters, pants, and skirts, thinking, *I really have nothing to wear*? You don't feel like ironing what's there. You try on one thing after another and feel unattractive in all of it. Proverbs 31:25 has the answer.

Strength and honor are the clothing of a virtuous woman. They never become wrinkled. They are always stylish, and they make any woman attractive. Best of all, instead of being purchased in an expensive department store, they are obtained and renewed by walking regularly with Jesus.

It may be true that as a mother of a little one you don't often feel clothed in strength, and after a battle of wills you might not feel especially honorable, but it's not your own strength and honor you should consider. It's God's. Let Him wrap you in godly garments, and you'll be the best-dressed mom around.

Dear God, remind me that being clothed in godliness
is much more effective than the new and expensive
but fading garments of this world. Amen.

The Perfect Mother

"My grace is sufficient for you, for my power is made perfect in weakness."

2 CORINTHIANS 12:9 NIV

John 15:5 (NIV) describes the type of living God planned for us: "I am the vine; you are the branches. If you remain in me and I in you, you will bear much fruit; apart from me you can do nothing." We are not expected to live any moment of life without the Lord. God desires for us to be in such close union with Him that the Holy Spirit in us lives *through* us. It is God in us that will enable us to not be perfect but to glorify Him as a mother. God requires us to lay down our inadequacies at the foot of the cross—our desperate pleas for help. It is then that God will make His grace sufficient for us. It is in our acknowledged weakness that God's power is made perfect and complete.

Lord, I desire to be in constant union with You. Holy Spirit, live life through me as I parent my child for Your glory. Amen.

Use Your Manners

*And a servant of the Lord must not quarrel but
be gentle to all, able to teach, patient, in humility
correcting those who are in opposition.*
2 TIMOTHY 2:24-25 NKJV

"Hey!" a toddler shouted at the pastor's wife, in an attempt to get her attention while she was welcoming visitors into the church. The boy's mortified mother quickly scolded him for his rude outburst.

"Hey!" that same mom shouted at her little boy, trying to get his attention in their backyard. She was shocked as she remembered scolding him in church for shouting the same word in effort to get someone's attention.

Children learn from their mothers how to treat others and what type of behavior is acceptable. We can enforce our rules and impose our desires on our children, but it would be much better to use our own good manners to model appropriate behavior.

Second Timothy 2:24-25 teaches us to be gentle to all and patient in our teaching. This includes when we teach our children.

---

*Jesus, please help me to be gentle and patient when
correcting my child. Let me be an example of You. Amen.*

Mother Hen

*"How often I have longed to gather your children together,
as a hen gathers her chicks under her wings."*

LUKE 13:34 NIV

A pastor told a story of how, when a new babysitter was hired, he would quietly pull the babysitter off to one side and remind her that all of the stuff he owned—the house, car, flat-screen television—could disappear while he and his wife were out. But if anything happened to his children, he said in all seriousness, well, she wouldn't want to know what would happen. His children were *that* valuable to him.

That is exactly how God feels about His children! He wants us all under His wing, safely cared for and lovingly protected. We are God's most prized possessions. So are our children. And our neighbor's children. Lost children. Lonely children. Even happy, well-adjusted children. God wants them all, every last one, under His wings of care. "He will cover you with his feathers, and under his wings you will find refuge" (Psalm 91:4 NIV).

Lord, teach me to care for others as You do. Help me not to grow weary or bored in praying for those around me. Amen.

Patient Endurance

We ourselves glory in you. . .for your patience and faith
in all your persecutions and tribulations that ye endure.

2 THESSALONIANS 1:4 KJV

God allows us to go through trials and struggles for a reason. He could do all things for us, but He has chosen not to. He knows we learn the most when the task is tough and we persist. God wants us to grow through our difficult experiences. Through these times, our faith deepens, and we have more appreciation for our Lord and who He is.

Our perseverance through tribulation also encourages others to know God and trust Him. When we look for the easy way out, we don't grow spiritually. We need to learn to have patience with our children as they practice and comprehend each new undertaking, and we need to have patience with God as He allows us to grasp more understanding of Him.

Jesus, You are the One I look to as I go through difficulties.
Help me to have patience and endure as You did. Amen.

I Love You the Most

"Love one another, even as I have loved you."

JOHN 13:34 NASB

At the close of each day, when tucking in their little ones, moms all over the world say, "I love you." What sweetness meets her ears when the small voice responds with, "I love you too, Mommy."

How wonderful of our heavenly Father to give us earthly examples of love. He, of course, is love itself, giving His only Child to die for people who didn't love Him in return. God the Father even had to turn His face from His Son, who took the sin of mankind on Himself. What unimaginable love! We tell Jesus we love Him, but He responds, "I love you more." He then commands us to love others in the same way that He loves us. How can we do any less for the One who loves us and gave His life for us?

---

*Lord, I thank You for loving me with such
an awesome love. Help me show others my
love for You by loving them more. Amen.*

Friendship

If either of them falls down, one can help the other up.
But pity anyone who falls and has no one to help them up.

ECCLESIASTES 4:10 NIV

God created us to be social creatures. We were made for relationship, with one another and with our Creator. Investing time in people results in having friends. Friends experience life together. They share joy and laughter, sorrow and pain. They celebrate victories and rejoice together in good times. They help carry life's burdens and lighten the load. Friends drop what they are doing to offer assistance. Friends put friends first. Friends lay down their lives for one another. All of which is extremely beneficial to a mother!

Take time to cultivate relationships. Get involved in your church and community to meet others. Make friendship a priority. Be the kind of friend to someone that you desire for yourself. Life is richer with a friend. It's never too late to begin establishing meaningful relationships with others.

Dear Lord, sometimes life is so busy that I
don't take the time to nurture relationships.
Help me make friendship a priority. Amen.

Chosen Satisfaction

But if we have food and clothing,
we will be content with that.
1 TIMOTHY 6:8 NIV

The mother sighed and closed her eyes, fighting impatience. Her child had whined all day. Nothing had satisfied her. She wondered if her daughter was coming down with something. Every time the girl was tired or getting sick, she was impossible to please.

Picking up her child, the mother held her close. The mother began to rock, hoping her daughter would forget her discomforts. The girl relaxed against her.

We are often cranky with God. The weather is too hot or too cold. Nobody likes us. We don't have enough money. People expect us to do everything. Work is piling up, and we don't have time to get our chores done. The complaints are endless.

Being satisfied, or content, is a choice. Our focus has to change from ourselves to God. We have to remember all He has done and given us. We must choose to focus on God and be satisfied with Him. We can lean back and relax in His arms.

Thank You, God, for helping me see the positives
of You and not the negatives of the world. Amen.

In His Time

He hath made every thing beautiful in his time: also he hath
set the world in their heart, so that no man can find out the
work that God maketh from the beginning to the end.

ECCLESIASTES 3:11 KJV

There's a fun children's song entitled "He's Still Workin' on Me." It has wonderful lyrics for both children and adults to claim. The only problem is that we tend to sing the words while ignoring the message.

It tells us not to judge our children yet because they're an incomplete work. God is still molding them just like He is us. No one is perfect yet, but that day is coming for those who have trusted Christ as their Savior. Only God knows when that day will be. Right now, we need to allow Him to do His work in our lives, and we should point our children in the right direction too. It is important to teach and discipline our kids, but we must do it with love and patience. Let's let God work in His time.

Father, I am imperfect and sometimes impatient, but I want to
let You work in Your time. Please grant me patience. Amen.

What Will Heaven Be Like?

"My Father's house has many rooms;
if that were not so, would I have told you that
I am going there to prepare a place for you?"

JOHN 14:2 NIV

Trying to understand heaven with our limitations would be like trying to explain to a fetus about life outside the womb. "Well, little baby, your lungs will fill up with air and you will start to breathe! And you'll be hungry and want to eat. Oh, and you'll feel hot and cold too. Trust me! You'll love it!" How could a fetus possibly understand? It's a realm beyond him. Given a choice, he might even prefer to stay where he is.

But we know more than a fetus knows. Jesus knows more about heaven than we can know. He gave us all of the information that we need: We belong in heaven, and a place is being prepared for us. We will live in God's presence forever.

If it were not so, Jesus would not have told us. Trust Him! You'll love it.

Lord of heaven, thank You for wanting
us to be with You for all eternity! Amen.

A Pure Heart

Maria had sent her little one, Paul, to a sleepover at his friend's house. Paul had come home the next morning, talking about dinosaurs eating people. Apparently, his friend's older brother had picked the movie for the evening. Maria had called over to the house. The friend's mother had apologized profusely, but that hadn't stopped Paul from waking them each night with nightmares.

Maria was just about to enter Paul's room, after being woken by his thrashing in bed, when she saw a sight that caused her to back away slowly from the door frame. Paul was leaning beside his bed, his hands clasped in prayer. "This is silly, God, because I know there are no monsters under my bed. I got brave enough this time and decided to check. Still, You have to protect me, okay? I'm just a boy. Thanks."

Paul climbed back into bed. Less than a minute later, he was snoring.

---

*Father, I praise You for giving me
a confident hope in You. Amen.*

Faith Is...

Now faith is confidence in what we hope for
and assurance about what we do not see.
HEBREWS 11:1 NIV

Faith is not wishful thinking, grasping at straws, or our last resort. Faith is taking God at His word. By faith, Noah built an ark, even though it had not yet rained. By faith, Abraham left his homeland and ventured to a foreign country, even though he could not see it. By faith, Moses led the people out of Egypt, even though he felt unqualified as a leader. These men of faith did not know what the future would hold, yet they knew the One who holds the future.

Faith requires a leap, a jump. Everything is not neatly figured out. If we had all the answers, faith wouldn't be required.

In response to what the Lord is asking us to do or believe, in faith, we simply say yes. We must trust God, knowing that He will keep His promises. We can stake our lives on His trustworthiness. Let's step out and believe Him. Let's exercise faith.

Dear Lord, give me faith to trust You when
I cannot see. Increase my faith. Amen.

*She opens her mouth in wisdom, and the
teaching of kindness is on her tongue.*
PROVERBS 31:26 NASB

From morning till night, Catherine spends the day interacting with her three young children. Her words, seasoned with grace, reflect patience, kindness, and gentleness. Unlike children who wilt under the stormy wrath of their parents, Catherine's children, like flowers turning toward the warm sunshine, experience daily nurturing through their mother's gentle assurance and guidance.

Catherine models Proverbs 31:26. Whether Catherine corrects or praises, she speaks in patient, quiet tones, words of faithful instruction. She has insight and good judgment because she is spiritually centered. She spends quiet time before the Lord each day before the children wake up. In addition, she seeks Him for wisdom throughout the day.

Do you desire to guide your children with words of wisdom, kindness, and faithful instruction? Then spend time with the Lord, pray, connect with other moms, and find a mentor. You will become that life-giving sunshine that reflects the source of true Light from our Savior.

---

*Holy Spirit, I invite You to fill me with Your words of wisdom,
kindness, and faithful instruction to my children. Amen.*

Proper Diet

*Jesus said to them, "My food is to do the will
of Him who sent Me, and to finish His work."*

JOHN 4:34 NKJV

Our children love to snack. Chips. Candy. Cookies. They love
foods that are tasty and quick to pop in their mouths. They
don't stop to consider the problems that come from indulging
in unwholesome fare. The young child only cares about eating
what tastes good at the moment.

We are often enticed into doing something other than
God's will. Sin can be very tempting, and some sins can seem
so small we don't realize we're "partaking" of an unhealthy
food. Just like our young charges, we can be so caught up in
our daily busyness, we don't stop to consider that we aren't
putting the right nourishment in our minds, spirits, and
bodies.

Let's make sure we're eating the right bread of life by
putting aside the temptation and getting the proper diet—
mentally, spiritually, and physically.

---

*Jesus, You have set the example for me. Thank You.
Help me to always do the Father's will and not my own. Amen.*

Thankful Hearts Pray

[I] cease not to give thanks for you,
making mention of you in my prayers.
EPHESIANS 1:16 KJV

Thankful hearts pray. When we understand that all that we have in this life comes from God, in whom "we live, and move, and have our being" (Acts 17:28 KJV), we will eagerly and gratefully run to Him.

On the other hand, if there are situations in our lives for which we are not thankful, we may be less likely to go to Him for help. If we have bitterness or unforgiveness or are discontent, we may not pray as we should.

Do we pray for our homes, even when they're cluttered? Our husbands, even when they are thoughtless? Our children, even when they misbehave?

We need to stop and be thankful for everything in our lives—the good and the not so good. And then lift up our requests, knowing He will answer our prayers and bless us, over and over again.

Thank You, Father, for these little children You have
given me. Thank You for entrusting them to me.
Please give me wisdom to direct them today. Amen.

The Promise Fulfilled

And so, after he had patiently endured,
he obtained the promise.
HEBREWS 6:15 KJV

God can be trusted to keep His promises in every area of our life—from meeting our needs, to giving us wisdom as we raise our children, to everything else. We know all of this, but too often we struggle because although we know He'll fulfill His promises, He doesn't always do it in our time frame.

Like Abraham and Sarah, many of us struggle with letting God work according to the schedule He has planned. We try to take matters into our own hands only to wind up with disastrous results. Think about all the trouble that Israel would have been spared had Abraham and Sarah not chosen to bring a baby boy into the world through their own time and means.

We must recognize that God really is God. He created and controls this universe. He sees the big picture and plans accordingly—and He always fulfills His promises.

Great God, You've never failed me. I know
You'll keep Your promises. Help me to
accept the timing You know is right. Amen.

Made for His Glory

And the Lord said unto him, Who hath made
man's mouth? or who maketh the dumb, or deaf,
or the seeing, or the blind? have not I the Lord?

EXODUS 4:11 KJV

The woman smiled encouragingly at the tiny baby with "special needs."

"Perfect in God's eyes," she told the mother.

Later that night, as the mother was rocking her daughter to sleep, the woman's words echoed in her mind.

Putting her lips next to her baby's ear, the mother whispered, "You, my angel, are perfect in God's eyes."

All children—those who have special needs and those who don't—have been designed for a special purpose. Through children and the challenges and joys they bring, imperfect mothers are molded into the image of Christ.

It's not always easy to accept our difficult situations, but it is God's sovereign plan.

And it is perfect.

Dear Father, although this situation is sometimes
difficult to accept, I thank You for this child and Your
perfect plan. Let Your Spirit flow through me to my
child, so together we will bring You glory. Amen.

Grow Up!

"You unbelieving and perverse generation,"
Jesus replied, "how long shall I stay with you?
How long shall I put up with you?"

MATTHEW 17:17 NIV

To Jennifer, this particular Sunday morning seemed the least holy morning of the week. The sweet rolls she'd been baking for Sunday school nearly set the oven ablaze while she had been refereeing a fight between three-year-old Madison and four-year-old Nick in the back bedroom. Hauling the teary children to church, Jennifer made the usual pre–Sunday school restroom stop. The bathroom exploded with Madison's screams. The church janitor had used bright blue freshener in the toilet!

Jennifer gritted her teeth. "When are you ever going to grow up?" Jennifer hung her head. How could she say such a thing to her children—at church, no less?

Many moms experience similar irritation and guilt when children act like—well, children! Jesus Himself, human as well as divine, sometimes struggled with immature, petty disciples. But He knew if He persevered, His followers would indeed grow up—and do great things for God!

Lord, help me see my children with Your eyes and trust
You for the energy to love them at this stage. Amen.

The Lord: An Everyday Experience

*These commandments that I give you today are to be
on your hearts. Impress them on your children. Talk about
them when you sit at home and when you walk along
the road, when you lie down and when you get up.*

DEUTERONOMY 6:6-7 NIV

Deuteronomy 6:4-9 provides the framework for making the
Lord an everyday experience for our children. As the Lord is
placed at the forefront of our minds and hearts, we are more
readily able to apply scripture to their lives.

The Christian market provides a number of helpful
ways—CDs, DVDs, books, and Bibles for children—to make
the Lord an everyday experience. Also, we may point out God's
beautiful creation and pray at set times (e.g., before meals,
naps, and bed) and spontaneous times (e.g., as we learn of a
friend in need) throughout the day. We can also sing praise
songs as a part of our nap time or bedtime routines. Soon,
our children will be making the Lord an everyday experience,
through prayer, praise, and song.

---

*Lord, enable me to make You an everyday experience
as I teach my child Your character and Word. Amen.*

The Barking Child

Every good and perfect gift is from above.
JAMES 1:17 NIV

God has made each one of our children a unique package, with different passions and talents. Often, a gift might be apparent in early childhood. A four-year-old might pretend to be an animal, driving her mom to distraction with barking dog sounds and cat meows, revealing her love of animals.

God set that passion for animals in that child's heart for a special reason. He's an animal lover too. It's possible that we may undervalue something God has set in our child's heart. Are we encouraging our children to persist in their areas of talent? Or do we try to steer them to what will pay the bills or provide security?

We need to help our kids make the most of the gifts God has given them—to practice those gifts and learn to employ them with patience and diligence. We want them to have a lifelong desire to use any talent—bug collector, cookie maker, tricycle racer—to serve God.

---

*Thank You, Lord, for creating such a unique package
of talents and abilities in my children! Help me
recognize Your ongoing work in their lives. Amen.*

Foundation of Righteousness

All Scripture is God-breathed and is useful for teaching,
rebuking, correcting and training in righteousness,
so that the servant of God may be thoroughly
equipped for every good work.
2 TIMOTHY 3:16-17 NIV

God's Word provides the tools we need to establish a foundation of righteousness in our children's lives. Second Timothy 3:16–17 tells us that we can use God's Word to teach, reprove, correct, and train in righteousness. This begins with a mom who knows God's Word, who searches His Word for the particular scriptures to use when correcting or praising her child's behavior, and who consistently applies scripture in her own life. For example, we can use God's Word in replacing a child's complaining, whining, and negative attitude by fostering and modeling thankful hearts (Philippians 2:14; Colossians 3:17; 1 Thessalonians 5:18). By using scriptures in ways like these, we can raise our child "in the training and instruction of the Lord" (Ephesians 6:4 NIV). Thus, God's Word establishes a foundation of righteousness in our household.

Heavenly Father, help me to be a student of Your Word.
Reveal to me how to apply scriptures in developing a
foundation of righteousness in my child. Amen.

A Rest from Work

For he spake in a certain place of the seventh day on this wise,
And God did rest the seventh day from all his works.

HEBREWS 4:4 KJV

As mothers, most of us have caught ourselves saying, "If only I had a few more hours. . ." Truthfully, if we had those hours, we'd quickly fill them and wish for more. There's no shortage of work for mothers.

Perhaps that is why we hesitate to take time to rest. Many moms are the first one up in their household and the last to go to sleep. But God knew we couldn't go on and on without ever taking a break, so He instituted a day for us to be physically and spiritually refreshed. It's tempting to fill those hours with draining activities too, but we have to realize that if we refuse to rest, the quality of our work, as well as our parenting, will suffer. Acknowledge this need, and find a way to accommodate it. Everyone will be better off when you do.

Father, it's not easy for me to take time to rest,
but it's needful. Help me add it to my to-do list. Amen.

Blessed be the Lord, Who daily loads us with benefits,
The God of our salvation!

Psalm 68:19 NKJV

Every day, God loads us with benefits. From sunrise to sunset, we have at our fingertips enough blessings to make us scream with delight and clap our hands. Be it joy in watching our little one discover something new, or pride in seeing them share with other children, or contentment in having everyone in our household happy and healthy. However, cares of the world and daily life can blind us to all that God has bestowed. We become weighed down with hardships, and we forget all about the wonderful aspects of being a believer in Christ.

We can choose to continue letting the negative aspects of the world steal our joy in God and His gifts, or we can turn around and see the heaping spoonful He is holding out to us. When we open our eyes to His blessings, our cares will fade away. God should have no doubt about our delight in Him.

You are my salvation, God. I thank You
and praise You for all You've done. Amen.

Don't Forget

In every thing give thanks: for this is the
will of God in Christ Jesus concerning you.
1 THESSALONIANS 5:18 KJV

Linn looked up at his mother. Today was Thanksgiving, and she had just read him the story of the first Thanksgiving. His thoughts turned to the turkey that had tasted so good. "Did the Pilgrims say grace before they ate their turkeys too?" he asked.

"Yes, they did," she said, nodding.

His four-year-old mind raced.

"Why?"

She yawned. "Why what?"

"Why did they say grace?"

"It had been a long, hard winter, and they were thankful that the Indians were sharing their food with them," his mother answered, resting her chin on top of Linn's head.

"Did they talk to Jesus all the time?"

"I think so," she answered. "They came to America so they would be free to worship God. Always remember to be thankful that the Pilgrims suffered so that we could talk to God any time we want."

Father God, thank You that my family is free to worship You
anytime. Thank You that I am free to tell my child about
You, and never let me forget to give You thanks. Amen.

Hot Potato

*Get rid of all bitterness, rage and anger, brawling
and slander, along with every form of malice.*

EPHESIANS 4:31 NIV

Remember the childhood game, hot potato? Participants tossed a ball to one another, pretending that it was a hot potato. The object was to get rid of the ball as quickly as possible. Holding on too long would result in your hands supposedly getting burned.

What things in life do we hold on to? We can dwell on an unkind word spoken by another. We can wallow in pain. Yet the Lord knows that holding onto these negative emotions can produce bitterness and anger. We may find ourselves desiring to hurt those who have harmed us. Yet in reality, we are the ones that eventually get burned.

So, like a hot potato, get rid of those negative thoughts as soon as you receive them. Give them to the Lord. Ask Him to restore your emotions by His grace. By doing so, the healing process can begin. Do not hold on and get burned. Get rid of the hot potato!

---

*Dear Lord, help me to quickly release
my hurt and pain to You. Amen.*

The Call to Home Missions

*But ye shall receive power, after that the Holy Ghost
is come upon you: and ye shall be witnesses unto me
both in Jerusalem, and in all Judaea, and in Samaria,
and unto the uttermost part of the earth.*

ACTS 1:8 KJV

Throughout her Christian life, the young mother had often heard the verses calling God's people to spread the Word: "Go ye into all the world" (Mark 16:15 KJV).

Yet with a preschooler, a toddler, and one more on the way, she could barely make it out of the house to shop, let alone go into the world to witness.

She called her mother in the faith. "How can I go up the road to witness to the neighbors when I have my hands so full with little ones?"

The older woman answered wisely. "This is the time in your life when you are called to home missions."

The young mother understood. Her home was her Jerusalem; her children, her personal disciples. Their souls were entrusted to her to nurture and guide.

---

*Faithful Shepherd of my soul, make me a tender and loving
shepherd to these little lambs You have given me. Amen.*

God's Divine Power

I have learned to be content in whatever circumstances
I am.... In any and every circumstance I have learned
the secret of being filled and going hungry, both of
having abundance and suffering need.
PHILIPPIANS 4:11–12 NASB

The apostle Paul was able to be content in whatever situations he endured (e.g., hungry or filled) because of his relationship with the Lord. He trusted and experienced God meeting every need (not want) that he had. Second Peter 1:3 (NIV) reads, "His divine power has given us everything we need for a godly life through our knowledge of him who called us by his own glory and goodness."

We have the ability to remain content by abiding in a daily relationship with the Lord, staying grounded in His Word, and communing with Him in prayer. As a mother of little ones, God will meet your needs and provide an eternal perspective on your circumstances. Trust His power for your contentment, and view your circumstances through His divine lenses.

Lord, help me to trust You to meet all of my needs and provide
an eternal perspective on my current circumstances. Amen.

Familiar Love

Herein is love, not that we loved God, but that he loved us,
and sent his Son to be the propitiation for our sins.

1 JOHN 4:10 KJV

Our love for our children does not depend on their behavior
or their gifts to us. We don't ask anything of them as payment
for caring for and loving them. Instead, we look at each child
as a gift from God, bestowed on us. We love with a depth of
emotion impossible to describe.

Likewise, God loves us more than we can comprehend.
He doesn't require anything in return. He loved us before we
even knew Him, before we understood the true definition of
love.

As we idly played or went on with our lives, God reached
out in love. He sent His Son, Jesus, to pay the penalty for our
sins, all because of the depth of feeling God has for us.

As we stop and watch our children and consider how
much we care for them, we can remember God does the same
with us. His heart is full as He gazes at us.

Thank You, God, that You love me
more than I can ever fathom. Amen.

Just a Handful

*Better is an handful with quietness, than both
the hands full with travail and vexation of spirit.*

ECCLESIASTES 4:6 KJV

Nora set down the newspaper and sighed disgustedly. "Celebrities have everything but common sense," she commented to her husband. "They have big, beautiful homes, perfect clothes, and more money than I can imagine spending; yet all they do is party, neglect their kids, and jump from spouse to spouse. What kind of life is that?"

"Shallow," Reid replied. "Makes you glad for our little two-bedroom house, doesn't it?" He grinned.

Nora smiled. Lately, she had been dropping hints that larger living quarters were needed. With two small children and a baby due soon, things were becoming rather cramped. Still, Nora knew that Reid was right. She was so thankful for her beautiful, happy children and her loving, faithful husband. She realized that God knew what was best when He designed His plan for her life. Nora thanked God for what her family had and for the joy and peace that filled their home.

*Thank You, Lord, for all Your blessings on my
family. When I'm tempted to complain, help me
to remember that Your gifts are perfect. Amen.*

God's Will

Now if we are children, then we are heirs—heirs of God and co-heirs with Christ, if indeed we share in his sufferings in order that we may also share in his glory.

ROMANS 8:17 NIV

Parents typically spend a lot of time and money when carefully considering what they will be able to leave their children when they die. That way, their children are left with no questions or doubts about what is coming to them or how to distribute it when the time comes.

Romans 8:17 is the will that our Father has left for us. He clearly defined how His estate would be distributed to ensure that there would be no mistaking the truth. We share as heirs in the kingdom of God with Jesus Christ, our Lord!

In order to reap the rewards of such glory, we must also share in the trials and tribulations that Christ endured. Just as Jesus did, we must also die to sin. We must take up our crosses and follow Jesus, enduring whatever we are called to bear along the way.

Thank You, Father, for my rich inheritance. Let me be Your servant, just as Christ served You. Amen.

Your Body

*Don't you realize that your body is the temple of the
Holy Spirit, who lives in you and was given to you by God?
You do not belong to yourself, for God bought you with
a high price. So you must honor God with your body.*

1 CORINTHIANS 6:19-20 NLT

Taking proper care of our bodies is as essential as taking care of our spirits. Getting enough sleep, eating nutritiously, and exercising to maintain optimal physical health are key elements to spiritual growth. Body and spirit are intertwined. How can we pray effectively or read God's Word if we are exhausted? How can we have energy at the end of the day for our children if our bodies are not properly nourished? How can we have stamina to participate on a mission trip if we're out of shape? Do not feel guilty for taking care of your body. Your spiritual life depends upon it!

---

*Dear Lord, so much of my time is spent meeting the needs of
my family. Help me realize the importance of taking care of
my physical body, and give me time to do so. Amen.*

Set a Playdate

So they left. . .for a quiet place,
where they could be alone.
MARK 6:32 NLT

If you're a mom, you're busy, right? However, a fast-paced schedule can become the focus of life, rather than the little ones whom we are raising. At times it's easy to absently reply, "Uh-huh," to a little one's rambling, without taking the time to stop and listen to the question or comment.

How about setting aside a morning and having a Mommy-and-me playdate with your child? Together, enjoy planning the special time, contemplating a meal location, an activity, or both.

When the special day arrives, mentally set this time aside for her exclusively. If you need to, turn off your cell phone. Take the time to listen to what she says, even if she does ramble. Take the time to be a kid again with her. Your full attention will speak volumes, and she will feel like the little princess that you consider her to be.

Lord, please help me to take the time to focus on my child.
As I take a few hours out of my busy schedule to give her
my full attention, bless our time together. Amen.

Do Something Great for God

*Therefore, I want younger widows to get married,
bear children, keep house, and give the enemy
no occasion for reproach.*

1 TIMOTHY 5:14 NASB

Good household management—the kind that follows the tenets of scripture—is one of God's main missions and privileges for women. Having children preserves us (1 Timothy 2:15). Loving and raising those children, loving and obeying our husbands, and managing our household preserves the testimony of the Lord (Titus 2:4–5). Showing hospitality to strangers and ministering to the needs of the saints is our fundamental God-given outreach (1 Timothy 5:10).

Being a dedicated mother and managing a household well, "as unto the Lord," is full-time Christian service because it is in the home and within family that the foundation is laid for salvation and where faith is passed on to future generations.

Such dedicated women do great things for God.

---

*Father, I get so busy with these little blessings You've
given me that I often do not see the big picture. Let me
raise my little ones and manage my household with
a passion for my family and for You. Amen.*

Dreary Days

He will make your righteous reward shine like the dawn,
your vindication like the noonday sun.

PSALM 37:6 NIV

Dreary days can be trying times for a mother. The weather isn't good, but your toddlers can't understand why they can't play outside. They get tired of staying indoors. Before long, you are as cranky as they are, praying for sunshine to relieve the boredom and stress.

Without fail, the sun will shine again. When it does, both mother and child are ecstatic. Those dismal times are quickly forgotten amid the joy of feeling the warm sun on your face.

In life there are times when one difficulty after another assails us. We feel battered and are unable to feel the warmth of God's joy. We long for relief, but we can't see an end to our trouble.

We need to cling to the hope we have in Christ. God will make the sun shine in our lives again as we trust Him. Trials pass. Good times come. We have hope and a reason to be thankful even in those dreary times.

Thank You, Jesus, for the hope You
bring us during trying times. Amen.

Recounting God's Faithfulness

*Posterity will serve him; future
generations will be told about the Lord.*
PSALM 22:30 NIV

God's Word encourages us to recount God's faithfulness,
particularly to our children (Psalm 78:4). It is essential for
our children to hear us describe how our Lord has been
trustworthy in performing wonders and miracles in our lives.
As our children hear us verbalize how God has worked for His
glory and our good (Romans 8:28), they will yearn to know
this dependable Lord. We are to record how the Lord has
worked "for a future generation, that a people not yet created
may praise the LORD" (Psalm 102:18 NIV). Our obedience in
recounting God's faithfulness will lead future generations
to know the Lord. This faithful Lord promises to keep His
covenant of love "to a thousand generations" (Deuteronomy
7:9 NIV) of those who love Him and keep His commandments.
We have the opportunity to influence a lineage of believers by
daily recounting God's faithfulness to our children.

---

*Lord, provide me with a heart that freely recounts Your
wonders in my life. I desire to create a lineage of
believers by my daily obedience to You today. Amen.*

*Since we are surrounded by so great a cloud of witnesses,
let us lay aside every weight. . .and let us run with
endurance the race that is set before us.*

HEBREWS 12:1 NKJV

How many times have we, as mothers, felt isolated and alone? We interact with our child or children, but that isn't the same as having a conversation with a friend. We long for company or just someone to talk to who doesn't depend on us. There can come a time when we are so down we don't feel we can endure the solitude anymore.

When we study all those in the Bible who have gone before us, we realize how much they sacrificed. Temporary isolation doesn't look so bad anymore. These people gave up much for God. For us to sacrifice our time for a few years doesn't look like much compared to what believers who have gone before us endured. When we are lonely, all we have to do is pick up God's Word and find the encouragement of the witnesses listed there.

*Lord, You have provided us with the inspiration of Your
followers. Thank You for them and their witness. Amen.*

Jesus' Clock

While he was still speaking to her, messengers arrived from the home of Jairus, the leader of the synagogue. They told him, "Your daughter is dead. There's no use troubling the Teacher now." But Jesus overheard them and said to Jairus, "Don't be afraid. Just have faith."

MARK 5:35–36 NLT

Jesus had agreed to go to Jairus's house to heal his sick daughter. On the way, Jesus was interrupted by a woman who boldly reached out to touch Him. Imagine Jairus's panic when Jesus stopped. Jesus wasn't in a hurry. He took time to speak to this woman, reassuring her that she was healed, then spoke to those around Him!

By then it was too late. Jairus's friends hurried to tell him his daughter was dead.

But Jesus' clock is different from ours. He knew all along that not only would the daughter's life be restored, but the sparks of faith alive in Jairus and his household would ignite into a flame that day.

It's never too late to invite Jesus into our homes and lives.

Lord Jesus, I pray that my children will enter into a loving and meaningful relationship with You—for life. Amen.

Pray as a Child

Be anxious for nothing, but in everything by
prayer and supplication, with thanksgiving,
let your requests be made known to God.

PHILIPPIANS 4:6 NKJV

Gloria dreaded this first Christmas without her loving hus-band. Since his death in the early spring, the money her loved one had left behind dwindled in their bank account. Matthew, her four-year-old, couldn't wait for Christmas. But Gloria was sure her ten-year-old daughter, Sarah, understood the strain she was under, because she hadn't mentioned gifts.

On Christmas Eve, Gloria asked Sarah to help get her brother ready for bed. She followed several minutes later to see how the kids were getting along. She stopped at the door to her son's bedroom. He and Sarah knelt beside the bed, and he prayed, "God, our mama isn't very happy, and I want You to make her happy. Thank You for giving us a good Christmas. Amen."

Gloria realized that both children knew how she felt and that they were praying for her. She went to her room, knelt by her bed, and let words of praise flow from her lips.

Dear heavenly Father, please teach me to
rely on You with a childlike faith. Amen.

Endure for the Joy

Looking unto Jesus the author and finisher of
our faith; who for the joy that was set before him
endured the cross, despising the shame, and is
set down at the right hand of the throne of God.

HEBREWS 12:2 KJV

Our Lord endured the rejection of the very people He came to save. And He endured the ultimate rejection of His Father as He became sin for us. Why did He withstand so much?

According to Hebrews, it was for the *joy* set before Him. He could see the ultimate victory—the salvation of man and His own restoration to His throne in heaven—so He patiently persevered in His task on earth.

A mother's life is also one of fortitude, enduring a multitude of tiny trials every day of her life. We must see our goal—godly children serving Christ and continuing in the faith for another generation.

Focused on that goal, we can endure with hope and joy.

Lord, You gave up much so that I could come to You. Give
me the patience to endure the trials of motherhood, so I
will have the joy of one day seeing them serve You. Amen.

My Spirit Rejoices

And my spirit hath rejoiced in God my Saviour.
LUKE 1:47 KJV

If you have accepted Christ as your Savior, His forgiveness is truly all you need to have a heart overflowing with praise to God, but in His goodness, our marvelous God grants us much more. Every woman's list is different. Perhaps yours includes a godly husband, beautiful children, and a comfortable home.

Mary was rejoicing in the amazing truth that she would soon give birth to the Savior of this world. That was a privilege no other woman would have. Still, God has given you the opportunity to raise up some of His other precious lambs, and that is cause to rejoice.

You might be tempted to focus on the troubles you have, but counting your blessings is much healthier. Certainly, Mary's opportunity was not without consequence. Her reputation and marriage were at stake, and she would eventually watch as her Son was murdered. Yet she still rejoiced that she was counted worthy to serve God. Are you rejoicing today?

---

*O Great Savior, I rejoice in the great work that
You do. You alone are worthy of praise. Amen.*

He Came to the Shepherds

*And there were shepherds living out in the fields nearby,
keeping watch over their flocks at night. An angel of the
Lord appeared to them, and the glory of the Lord shone
around them, and they were terrified.*

LUKE 2:8–9 NIV

Are we open to receive the Good News? Jesus was born so that we could live. He came to give us eternal life by paying the penalty of our sin through His death. By faith we are forgiven and redeemed. Do we have eyes to see our need of a Savior? Do we have ears to hear the Gospel message?

May we learn from the shepherds. Away from the hustle and bustle of the crowds, they had quiet time to reflect, ponder, and pray. Humility and contentment characterized their lives. They were not puffed up with knowledge and religiosity, judging others that did not measure up. The Lord made a bold statement by appearing to the shepherds. May we grasp the message and have hearts to receive Him.

---

*Dear Lord, may my heart be humble so I acknowledge my
need of You each day. May I revel in the Good News! Amen.*

God's Valuables

*And they shall be mine, saith the LORD of hosts, in that
day when I make up my jewels; and I will spare them,
as a man spareth his own son that serveth him.*

MALACHI 3:17 KJV

"It's all about me."

In Old Testament times, God's people swallowed this
idea. In fact, they believed that God had given them a raw
deal. He hadn't met their expectations of prosperity. They
viewed themselves as righteous victims who followed God's
laws and suffered, while evildoers achieved success.

God slashed through their false veneer to reveal the
truth: His people had deserted Him. They followed other
gods. They stole each others' spouses. They robbed God and
His workers of monetary support and deprived helpless
widows and orphans of justice. They mistreated people from
other ethnic backgrounds.

But a few genuine believers remembered they were
created to love and serve God, not indulge their appetites.
They stuck together and honored Him.

God held these believers like rare, sparkling jewels
in His hand and promised He would spare them the total
devastation reserved for their hypocritical countrymen.

---

*Father, please keep me in Your love
and guide me in Your ways. Amen.*

A Lifesong of Joy

Satisfy us each morning with your unfailing love,
so we may sing for joy to the end of our lives.

PSALM 90:14 NLT

Webster defines joy as "the emotion evoked by well-being, success, or good fortune." Can you recall the last time you experienced true joy?

As a mom, joy can at times seem a distant emotion. When you are tired and have just folded the third load of laundry of the day, how can there be joy? Stop for a moment and think about the precious treasure who wore those jeans while chasing a butterfly or who donned that sweatshirt to go jump in the leaves outside.

In 1 Thessalonians 5:16 (NLT), we are told to "always be joyful." That doesn't mean we are to be giddy when things go wrong. Rather, God desires that we maintain a spirit of joy, resting in Him.

A joyful spirit is contagious. Find delight in the "ordinary" moments, and others will catch the joy.

Lord Jesus, please be my source of joy today,
even when I'm tired or things don't go quite right.
Let me rest in the fact that You are in control. Amen.

Learn to Be Merry

Is any among you afflicted? let him pray.
Is any merry? let him sing psalms.
JAMES 5:13 KJV

God does not promise that the minute we accept Him our lives will be without trial. It is also not His intention that when trials come we mope around or worry. This is where faith and prayer come into play. Is your child prone to illness? Seek His wisdom in how to handle the situation. Is your child's behavior difficult at best? Realize that God has dealt with many hard cases and has a wealth of wisdom to share.

Don't get caught up in the tough circumstances. You are a child of the all-powerful God. Let Him handle the problems. Begin looking for reasons to rejoice. Find humor in situations. Concentrate on God's blessings and offer praise to Him as you begin to notice them. Soon you will be so filled with His joy that you will not have reason to concentrate on the difficulties.

Lord, I'm often tempted to complain. Help me instead to turn my trials over to You and to learn to rejoice. Amen.

Your Little Will Grow, But You'll Still Be on the Go. . .

3-Minute Prayers for Moms

This devotional prayer book packs a powerful dose of inspiration into just-right-sized readings for moms of all ages and stages. Each prayer, written specifically for devotional quiet time, meets readers right where they are—and is complemented by a relevant scripture and question for further thought.

Paperback / 978-1-68322-417-4 / $5.99